For my sister, who lights up every room she
walks into. Never stop shining!

Acknowledgements

I would like to express my deepest gratitude to my birth mother who gave me life and to my parents who taught me how to live it!

Shout-out to all of my fellow adoptees. While our stories may vary, in many ways we are the same. I see you and honor you.

Special thanks to Judy Kane for encouraging me to journal my story and turn it into a book. Thank you for your continuous love and support.

Big thanks to Michelle Khouri for her phenomenal editing skills!

Much gratitude to Nuri Keli for designing the cover of this book.

Thanks to Pedro Pestana Kogake for helping with my author photo and book formatting.

Thank you to all of the people who have supported me along my journey in big ways or small. You helped make this book possible.

This book is a work of creative nonfiction. The events are portrayed to the best of Mariela Andersen's memory. While the stories in this book are true, some names have been changed to protect the privacy of the people involved.

Home Sweet Casa:
A Journey to the Universal Heart

by Mariela Andersen

INTRODUCTION

Imagine never knowing a single person who shares your genetic code. Imagine never having the opportunity to recognize the shape of your brow or color of your eyes or curvature of your chin in someone else's face. I'm sure it's an easy blessing to take for granted. This hypothetical was in my case, a reality. After my first breath outside of the womb, I did not see my birth mother's face again for 19 years.

I was adopted at five weeks old by Lisa and Pete, a loving and generous American couple that would dedicate their lives from that point forward to molding me into a sympathetic and caring young adult. Being given up for adoption and subsequently adopted never felt like a burden. My mom and dad adopted three children from the same orphanage in Colombia at three separate times through an agency called The Barker Adoption Foundation. My two brothers, and I enjoyed privileged and joyful childhoods. We tormented each other, we laughed together, we created family rituals and overcame times of hardship. We flourished, as any family does, in a peaceful and stable home held together by honesty, trust and love--not genetic coding.

I have fond memories of singing and clapping along with my parents, who would stand over my bed as soon as my teeth were brushed and the covers had been tucked tightly at my sides, to celebrate my origin story. Through a gleaming smile topped by shining eyes, my mom would sing "You're adopted! You're adopted!" What a profound impact this would go on to have. If one theme has unfolded throughout my life it's just how misunderstood adoption is, at least in American society. And not just in one way. Misconceptions surrounding adoption--what it is, what it means, how it shapes families and adoptees--come in many flavors. In fifth grade, my classmates asked me if I used to sing songs out of the orphanage window like Little Orphan Annie. Even as a child, I found that thought ridiculous. I never considered myself "an orphan." In fact, I referred to my orphanage (la Fundación para la Asistencia de la Niñez Abandonada, or FANA) as my "adoption home." Questions like that instilled in me a subtle "otherness" from a young age, and the overall awareness that, in all actuality, I was an orphan during the first few weeks of my life. And yet, I'm lucky enough to say I've never felt unwanted or abandoned. My story never filled me with shame or profound sadness. I have Lisa and Pete to thank for that. After all, why should it?

In Lisa and Pete--my mom and dad--I see my tendency to give and my endless capacity for love. And while my parents have gifted me with an abundance of learned traits, I couldn't look less like them. Tall and thin, my father's fair complexion and delicate features are a billboard for his Scandinavian lineage. He met his wife, my beautiful mother, when he was 20 and she was 16. He was a junior in college and had befriended her brother. He stopped by her childhood home one day to meet up with her brother and was enamored the second he saw her walking nonchalantly down the stairs. Apparently, she couldn't have cared less--the teenage condition, I guess. Years later while attending the same college they would re-connect and fall in love and the rest as they say, is history.

As a child, my gaze would often fall on my mother while she did house chores or readied my school lunch. I would admire her brown hair, straight and fine, and the way her delicate figure exemplified the curves of the female form. I would naturally compare myself to my parents, contrasting myself with their light skin, delicate features and slender frames. Meanwhile, my reflection showcased the genetic riches of another world.

Thick, dark hair cascades from my head like a tangle of vines. A wide nose, strong chin and plump lips take up the most real estate on my rounded face, while my hooded and expressive eyes are dead giveaways for my South American bloodline. At five feet tall, my petite-yet-powerful frame is supported by thick thighs and strong arms. The first time I saw a picture of the Colombian pop star Shakira, I felt taken aback by how many of my own features I saw in her. I would later learn Shakira shares the same hometown--and characteristic features--as my birth family.

And so, while I was raised with the kind of family many kids dream of having, our inescapable physical differences became daily reminders of this mysterious group of people out there, somewhere, who shared different variations of my genetic building blocks. This primordial longing to meet those who share my bloodline would linger in my mind like a tiny gray cloud in a vast blue sky--until the day I turned 19.

CHAPTER ONE
Searching

My adoption was a "closed adoption", which means my parents never met my biological mother and she wasn't involved in my life. I did, however, grow up with open access to my adoption files. My mom kept the files like any family safeguards their memories, in a shoe box on the top shelf of our entryway closet. Whenever I wanted to flip through the pages that documented my beginnings, I could tug at my mom's shirt and the box would materialize.

I was raised with only one rule regarding my adoption. According to Colombian law, adoptees must be 18 years of age or older to start the search for their birth family. Parents of minors can act as guardians of the search if an adoptee under the age of 18 wants to find their birth parents. My parents stood firm on their belief that my brothers and I should manage the search ourselves if or when the time came. Thus, I was to wait until my eighteenth birthday if I ever felt the urge to search for my birth family. It's as if that lone rule turned any desire I had to meet my birth mother into a sleeper agent that lay dormant in my subconscious. And so, at age 19, I felt a sudden urge to find a clear picture of the woman who gave birth to me.

On April 27, 2009, with an inquisitive mind and slightly trembling hands, I addressed an email to FANA's general email address.

Hello,

My name is Mariela Andersen. I was adopted from FANA in 1990. My parents told me that there were pictures of children's birth parents on a wall at FANA, but you had to be 18 in order to see them. I am now 19 and I don't have the funds to travel to Colombia, but I was wondering if there was a way to see the picture of my birth mom.

I am not currently interested in tracking her down and meeting her; however, I am curious as to what she looks like. If you cannot help me with this, then that is fine. I would still love to hear more about where I came from. Thank you

Weeks and multiple follow-up emails flew by, giving me enough time to create my own imaginary version of my birth mom's face. And finally, on June 6th, the fateful email came through harboring in its attachments the picture I felt I'd waited a lifetime to see. There I was. In her dark, intense eyes. In the curls of her dark hair. In the width of her nose and the heaviness of her eyelids. I put a hand to my face, as if to feel her features through my own. Tears streamed over and around my fingers, and my heart thumped rapidly, rhythmically. In that moment, it felt as if I was made entirely of heartbeats and tears. Along with her image, my contact at FANA sent the background information my birth mother submitted upon her arrival at the orphanage in 1990. With each word, it was as if the expressionless face staring at me from her black-and-white photo gained a jolt of life. The email has been lightly edited for spelling and grammar, where necessary. After all, there is a language barrier. And this won't be the last time that barrier rears its frustrating head.

Dear Mariela,

I have your file in front of me and I will tell you what it says about your birth mother from the information she gave to one of our social workers years ago.

She first came to FANA on January 31, 1990, when she was about seven months pregnant. FANA gave her pre- and post-natal care, like FANA has done since it was founded 37 and a half years ago. She was born in a town named Contratacion, located in the State of Santander, on May 1, 1970. She had dark brown hair, brown eyes, medium complexion. She mentioned that her own parents were separated for about eight years. She was the fourth of seven children. She did not have a good relationship with her family, and they did not know she was pregnant.

Your birth father was a man she met and dated for about a year. When he found out she was pregnant, he abandoned her and she never heard from him again. She said she wanted to give you up for adoption because she was a young woman who felt she could not be responsible for you alone. She did not want you to suffer in life. She wanted you to have a family that she did not have, being single. She said that your birth father was 24 years old and going to school [while they were dating]. She said he had dark hair, dark eyes, and a medium complexion.

Your birth mother, like the thousands of birth mothers that have come to FANA, always make a tremendous sacrifice of love by giving their children up for adoption. They give their children the right to life and the right to have a family like you have had. I hope this information will answer some of your natural wonders.

I felt overwhelmed and overjoyed. I took a picture of myself mimicking her expression in the photo and placed them side by side. The resemblance was uncanny. I uploaded the side-by-side image to Facebook to share the landmark occasion with my friends. One by one, comments poured in as my friends lent their support of an extraordinary first step that would soon lead to a life-changing journey.

In my email to FANA, I mentioned having no interest in "tracking her down." As you might imagine, that disinterest quickly disappeared after I received my birth mother's photo and the accompanying snapshot of biographical information. The search for my birth mother had more going for it than many other adoptees. I was lucky enough to have easy and open communications with my orphanage, which kept pristine records. I had a picture of my mother, and could assume she was still living in Bogotá, Colombia's capital city. See, in Colombia, economic opportunity lives in Bogotá. In fact, middle- and lower-class Colombians in search of financial stability have no option but to call Bogotá home. I set out to find her, at first using online resources and word of mouth connections that led to several dead-ends. It was easy to find people who wanted to help, but much more difficult to find those who could actually bring me closer to my mission. Time passed as the search came to a halt. Two years later, at the ripe age of 21, I decided to start searching again and made full use of the near-limitless tools offered by social networking sites. I began building a network of Colombian adoptees through chat rooms and forums. I joined a Facebook group called "Adopted from Colombia," or AFC, and it wasn't long after that my trail of breadcrumbs landed me at my long-desired destination.

There are over 2,000 Colombian adoptees on this page, who live all over the world, including in Norway, Sweden, Spain, Australia, and throughout the United States. This Facebook page acts as a digital support group where members share their origin stories, how they found their birth families, and their hopes for locating them. Others express not wanting to find their birth families, as well as feelings of guilt, shame, resentment or anger surrounding their circumstances. One adoptee told me how he found his birth mom. When he traveled to Colombia to meet her, he was shaken to see her home had dirt floors, no windows and no doors. I chatted with another adoptee living in Israel, an adult man who had only recently found out he was adopted. Some shared stories about their adoptive families, growing up with abusive or narcissistic parents who expected praise for having adopted them. Or, they felt the adoptee owed them for 'rescuing' them from their prior circumstances. There is a whole other Facebook group dedicated to adoptees raised in such households. Others share heartbreaking stories of looking for their biological families only to find out they were victims of child trafficking, kidnapped and illegally put up for adoption without their birth mother's consent. What a wealth of stories, backgrounds, cultures and individuality this group represented. And still, we are bonded under the strength of one uniting experience--an experience that shapes us all differently, but that nonetheless leaves its unmistakable mark.

In this group I found a "family" of like-minded people who helped me to reconcile that subtle "otherness" I felt since childhood. And maybe most importantly, in this group I found a network of reliable detectives.

* * *

It so often seems that life's greatest moments trail behind periods of rock-bottom despair. Such was the case for my search. Riddled with twists and turns that left me feeling dejected by false hopes and dead ends, I decided to step away from my search for a few weeks. Only a short time later, a friend from the AFC group referred me to Carolina Gonzalez, a Colombian woman who does family searches for a living. I felt my patience and hope dwindling, and so in a last-ditch expression of faith, I reached out to Carolina and presented my case. I explained I couldn't pay her for her services, almost certain she would turn me away since we all need to make a living. To my great surprise (and in hindsight, the first sign of serendipity), Carolina agreed to take on my case free of charge since I would be her first U.S.-based client. In return, I readily agreed to refer her to adoptees living in the U.S.

And since expectations so often breed disaster, I sent Carolina my adoption paperwork and braced myself for any result--good or bad. Encouraged by so many past disappointments, I erased all dreams of a specific outcome from my mind, but kept my fingers crossed. Having zero expectations, after all, is certainly easier said than done.

Carolina called two weeks later. *Deep breaths.* She had big news. *Breathe, Mariela.* The day had come, she said. She found my birth mother. I froze. This wasn't the first time I had received this news. I wanted to be sure she made contact with the right person. And what if she was, in fact, my birth mother but wanted nothing to do with me? My mind raced. Then, Carolina informed me: this *was* my birth mom and she was *ecstatic* to hear about me. She wanted to meet me. My heart pounded out of my chest as the reality set in--we did it. We found her. And now, the hardest part of all.

I seized the moment to video call Carolina in Colombia, who then called my birth mom, María, on speaker phone. The other line crackled, fading in and out, but I could hear her. *Is this really happening?* I could make out my birth mother's voice as she muttered in Spanish through tears. Until that point, I had been so fixated on finding my birth mom that I had never given much thought to the potential language barrier. I wasn't prepared for the gaping divide in communication caused by our different cultures. And so, I was left grasping for context clues in a moment when all I wanted was to hear every syllable this person who gave birth to me had to say, and in turn ask her what felt (and still feels) like an endless number of questions.

That's when Andrea came to the rescue. My friend Andrea is Latina and speaks Spanish fluently. She just so happened to be at my house when Carolina delivered the results of this life-changing search. Serendipity once again saved the day. Andrea jumped in when she saw me struggling to catch the conversational clues of an unfamiliar language. But a spotty Internet connection left my friend-turned-interpreter struggling to understand what María was saying. All the while, I stared at the screen wide-eyed and bounced up and down from the sheer joy of it all. "I wish you could see Mariela right now, because she is so beautiful," Carolina exclaimed to María. Andrea translated as my birth mom then shared the story of my birth. "The nurses said she looked like a doll," said María through tears. "She was very beautiful." My birth mom was gushing about me, her daughter. There I was, at 21 years old, hearing for the first time about the moment I greeted the world. I'd never felt so equally euphoric and stunned.

"Tell her I'm sorry. Tell her I only did it to give her the best possible life," María kept saying over and over. She wept each time she uttered these words, and in these moments, I didn't need an interpreter to know that my birth mother was plagued by guilt.

I asked Andrea to console her. "Tell her I have never been mad at her. Explain that I have always been grateful and understanding of her decision to put me up for adoption." I wished more than ever I could connect with her directly in this moment. Asking others to relay your heartfelt sentiments inevitably waters down those feelings, filters them. Once Carolina translated this message, María expressed some relief. "I want to hold her. I want to ask for her forgiveness in person," she told Carolina. "I hope she can find it in her heart to forgive me one day." I tried again and again to convey that, far from angry or resentful, I had instead always felt immense gratitude to my birth mother for making what I could only gather to be an excruciating decision to give up her first-born child. Still, no matter what I said to reassure her, she clung unrelentingly to her guilt like the lifelong burden it had been. My birth mother then told me her birthday was just the day before. "Thank you for giving me the best gift I could have ever asked for," she said through Carolina.

There we sat, lifetimes, oceans, cultures and languages apart, and yet it seemed all we could do was revel in this unlikeliest of reunions. Finally, it was time to end the call. My heart sank as I said goodbye, only to lift again as gratitude filled every part of me like helium and sent me soaring. And to think this was just the beginning.

That evening, I sat on the front stoop of my house processing the conversation I had just shared with my birth mother. My parents pulled into the driveway while I lingered on the doorstep of contemplation. "I need to tell you something," I said wearily. I asked them to sit down, at which point I explained that I had just made contact with my birth mother, who, as it turned out, was thrilled to hear from me. "She wants to meet me in person," I said. My father's eyes filled with tears as he congratulated me. "I'm so happy for you, Mari," my mother said, holding me tightly. Her hug lingered longer than usual, and I could hear her breathing grow heavy through our embrace. My mom later admitted she spent quite a few sleepless nights worrying my birth family would reject me if I ever found them. Even as she said this, I felt something linger around her, like a gray aura of concern, but I was too overcome by the day's overwhelming emotions to decipher what it was that hung around us that night.

As the night drew to a close, thoughts kept flooding my mind about the experiences that had filled the previous hours. With little desire to go to bed, I went instead to my friend Juan's house. Juan is Colombian, so it's probably no small coincidence that I decided to visit him that night. To my surprise, when I arrived, he grabbed me by the arms and exclaimed, "Let's call your birth mom! I'll translate!"

"Juan, it's 11 p.m. She might be sleeping," I urged him to reconsider (half-heartedly, because I really did want to call her). It didn't take much insistence from Juan to get her on the phone. Within seconds, María was on the other end. This time, we were having what felt like a normal conversation, thanks to a solid phone connection and Juan's smooth translations. During this conversation, I found out that my birth mother was not the one who named me. My parents had long ago told me they kept my Colombian name to honor my birth mother. I always felt connected to her through my name, even if only slightly. María explained that we were only together for a moment after she gave birth to me. She didn't even have a chance to see what gender I was. I was born and seconds later, the nurses swept me away to care for me to ensure it was not too painful an experience for María. "That was the last time I saw her," she cried to Juan, whose own eyes welled with tears. As it turned out, nurses and social workers at the orphanage typically name the babies, so I can only assume that is how I received my own name. Either way, I am grateful. I like my name. Hours after I was born, one kind nurse was empathetic enough to sooth María's anxious heart by telling her she had given birth to a beautiful baby girl, who looked like a doll.

Juan's room pulsed with a powerful energy while we spoke, accompanied only by the sound of crickets outside his window. Juan listened with glistening eyes to the weeping voice on the other end. Only one set of eyes remained dry in the house--mine. I cried many times before finding María. I grew up fantasizing about meeting my birth mother. I wept out of fear that she would reject me. I cried hoping she was still alive. But now, when finally, those dreams were becoming a reality, it's as if the well had run dry. I felt blank. What I didn't know then was that this was the face of shock. As it turns out, my emotional blank-slate experience is a common one for adoptees. When you are faced with such a flood of feelings and thoughts to process, it's like your brain's only option is to implement an emotional override. A system reset.

I tried to let myself off the hook for not succumbing to the moment in the same way María, Carolina and even Juan did. Instead, I focused on absorbing as much information as I could. And so, the cycle of translation continued, with Juan bestowing on me bits of mind-blowing information followed by silence as he listened intently to the next piece of the puzzle my birth mother provided him. Patience was never more a virtue than during those moments of silence.

* * *

"You have a four-year-old sister. Her name is Lorena Sara, but everyone calls her Sara," said Juan. My mouth fell open. I always dreamed of having a sister. I grew up the only girl, a middle child between two brothers. "She thinks you probably look alike, because when Sara was born the nurses said she looked like a doll, too" he continued, listening to the bits and pieces coming to him from the other end of the phone. I was beside myself. The smile that was already dominating my face, grew impossibly larger. But that was just the beginning. "You have a younger brother, too! Santiago. He's 18," Juan's excitement grew with each new revelation. She told Juan she had not yet broken the news of my existence to my half siblings. She said she needed time to sort out how she was going to tell them. This led her to explain that, at that point, the only person who knew about me was her husband, Vincente. María mentioned wanting to tell her sister Cristina before anyone else, because of the close bond they've always shared. Unfortunately, Cristina was in China on business, so breaking the news would have to wait for her return. Impatience got the best of me as I worried how long it would take for my whole birth family, and especially my half siblings, to learn about me.

All that worry turned out to be useless, when not 24 hours later I received a Facebook friend request from someone named "Santi Jimenez"--my brother. I messaged him immediately upon accepting his request, and we began chatting in a surprisingly natural and familiar way. I felt an instant connection and even love for him. I looked through his Facebook page and my heart melted when I saw a photo of my baby sister, Sara. In a matter of days, I went from never having seen a face that looked like mine, to a whole family of similarly featured people unfolding before my very eyes. Santiago and I look especially alike. We share nearly identical noses and lips. And, Sara! In the first-ever picture of her I saw, her hands were planted firmly on her hips, her powerful spirit on full display, and her lips curled into a coquettish smile--the same smile I have seen in my mirror many times. My heart pounded as I saw my features reflected back to me. A bizarre, thrilling and illuminating experience, to say the least.

All the while, I continued Facebook messaging with Santiago, whose English was equally as broken as my Spanish. "I have an idea," I told him as I sent him the link to an online translation software in hopes of helping the conversation go more smoothly. What had already been a slow conversation crawled to a snail's pace, as we each made the effort to send messages in each other's native tongues. Impatience once again bubbled to the surface. All I wanted to do was fluidly speak to this "new" family.

"I want to learn English," he typed with the Internet's help. "I want to learn so I can talk to you better." My heart must have grown three times its size when he said this. In that moment, the desire to meet my birth family became a nearly unbearable necessity. I promised him I would come and visit Colombia when I had the means to do so.

* * *

The day after Santiago and I first connected, I eagerly awaited the green circle to appear next to his name indicating his logged-in status. All I could think about since first "meeting" him was learning everything about him. How does he spend his days? What was his childhood like? What are his hobbies? How does he feel about this lifelong secret his mother kept from him? The green dot lit up next to his name, and so did my spirits. One video call later, and I was looking at my brother face to face for the first time in my life. We sat there and smiled for a few moments, both of us processing the magnitude of this connection. The conversation didn't last long. Santi is a young man of few words and fewer emotional nuances. As if that wasn't enough, he was in an Internet café, which meant his time was limited and the connection was unstable. Regardless, I will remember every second of that short-lived video call for the rest of my life.

Later that night, I visited my friend Juan, who once again agreed to call María with me and translate our conversation. "Tell her Santiago was so happy to talk to her," she told Juan. "Half of his school already knows about his sister in the United States! He can't wait to show her off to his classmates and cousins," she told him. María then asked if I really would visit them in Bogotá. I could tell she was nervous I would not follow through on my promise. After all, we had just met, and while the familial connection seemed to be growing more rapidly than I could have ever dreamed, we still knew so little about each other. Namely, we had not yet gotten to know one another's character and values. "Tell her this is something I have always dreamed of doing. I'll find a way," I said to Juan.

"Tell her...," I hesitated as my throat tightened. "Tell her that before I found her, I used to look longingly at the moon. It made me feel close to her, knowing we were under the same sky. I'd turn my gaze upward on clear nights and imagine she was looking up at the same moment. All I have ever wanted was to be able to sit under that very moon beside her," I told Juan. He took a deep breath, and translated.

Before hanging up that night, Juan handed me the phone and, for the first time, I talked to my birth mother directly, without a translator. We repeated "I love you" over and over. I could hear how happy she was; I could practically feel her love for me coursing through my veins. A rush of blood gave my heart a few extra beats.

The next day was Cinco de Mayo. In the U.S., May 5th is primarily an opportunity for binge drinking and party hopping. Instead, I hunkered down in front of my computer waiting to see that little green dot pop up next to Santiago's name on Facebook. I bit away at my fingernails as an hour turned into two, which turned into three. My cursor hovered over the "Close" button, but before I could give up on talking to him, the green light appeared, and I received a video call. Not only was Santiago smiling at me from my computer screen, but so were María and Sara. Their dad, María's husband Vincente, was in the background waving. I felt euphoric as we began trying to communicate without the help of an interpreter.

With my lack of Spanish fluency, much of the conversation went misunderstood. What I did make out, though, was that Sara was apparently named after me. According to my birth mom, she had wanted to name me Lorena Sara when I was born. Since the nurses took me away before she could name me, my little sister became my semi-namesake. Sara then shouted "¡Hola!" and counted to 10 in English. I saw that charming smile I had only seen in photos at that point, and that's all it took for little Sara to capture my heart. "¡Muy bien!" I responded, wishing I could accompany my "job well done" with a tight hug. We navigated the rest of the conversation through half-understood phrases and unflinching smiles. My birth family showered me with compliments--to them I was endlessly intelligent and beautiful. As it turned out, spoken language became less of a barrier and more of a footnote; love became a sufficient form of communication. When it finally came time to say *adios*, I sat in sad stillness for a while. *I have to find a way to visit them*! I thought.

Santiago and I connected again on Facebook that night. It seemed as if I was growing more restless each time we chatted online. He was slow to translate his messages and would not accept my offer to translate them myself. To add to that frustration, it looked like the excitement of our new relationship was starting to wear off for Santi, whose answers were getting shorter and less detailed as time wore on. *Is it me? Does he just not like me?* I asked about his thoughts and feelings, but he would change the subject every time. I told myself it was the language barrier, but my intuition knew he didn't know how to open up. Or maybe he didn't *want* to open up...to *me*. Maybe I got ahead of myself thinking this was a fairytale come true. Self-doubt has a swift way of dismantling both hope and optimism.

I decided to confront these feelings head-on the following night. When Santiago logged on, I asked him why his responses were growing shorter, more distant and sparser with time. He assured me that, like his mother, he is a person of few words. "I am a woman of many words. I wonder who gave me my talkative genes," I retorted jokingly. I don't think he found it funny. I went to bed that night plagued by insecurity. Was I being too loving toward him? Was I inadvertently pushing my brother away? *He's just a kid*, I told myself. *I'm sure he loves me. He just doesn't know how to express it.*

At some point, I had grown far more concerned with getting to know my half siblings than my birth mother. I was so interested in having a relationship with Santi and Sara that, at times, it even felt more exciting than talking to María. I wish there was a rulebook for finding your birth family. I wish someone could have just told me how to feel. What kind of emotional responses are considered "normal" in this type of situation? My only option was to figure it out as I went.

* * *

Throughout the weeks that followed, I dedicated all of my focus to finding ways to make enough money to visit Bogotá. In those same weeks, I was brought in contact with several members of my birth family. We connected face to face on the webcam and exchanged photos and videos through Facebook. One after another, each new person I met would comment on how much I look like the family. This and a thousand other thoughts raced through my head. Every day I was learning more about who I was and where I came from. My life was changing right before my eyes.

Truths about my birth family and my adoption continued to reveal themselves as the months passed. I learned María makes a living as a cook. She takes orders every day for the next day's lunch, then prepares and personally delivers all of the meals in the shopping center where several members of the family work selling shoes. During one conversation, María mentioned that Santiago had always felt like a part of his mom was missing and could never explain why...until now. He seems happy that María and I found each other, but that's just an educated guess. I continue to find it hard to decipher, let alone understand, Santi's true feelings.

A separate video call with my birth mom revealed that Sara struggles with a congenital disease in which one kidney is larger than the other. "It is expensive to treat but we do everything we can to get her the care she needs," explained

María. My heart sank at the thought of Sara suffering. I learned Santiago didn't want to go to college, and that Vincente was a taxi driver. I learned Sara loves watching Disney cartoons, and that she didn't yet know the full story about who I was and how I came to be. I learned that Latinas celebrate their fifteenth birthdays with *quinceañeras,* over-the-top parties that are a sacred cultural tradition. I learned that on my fifteenth birthday, María secretly celebrated my *quinceañera* by paying for a church to hold mass in my honor. The puzzle pieces about my newfound family were steadily interlocking. Each conversation seemed to bring me closer to closing the 20-year gap that divided us. The one thing--or rather, person--no one seemed to want to address was my birth father. I was too preoccupied with the new family tree blossoming before me to notice the missing branch.

CHAPTER TWO
Processing

I quickly became engulfed by the idea of growing relationships with my birth family. Balancing every other relationship in my life seemed impossible, and at a minimum a chore. I broke up with my boyfriend of four years during this time. Hindsight now gives me the clarity to understand that when I opened the door to this never-before-known world of connection, I unknowingly tinted every other relationship with new perspective. I suppose a part of me always looked for relationships to compensate for this missing family, even though I grew up in a happy and full home where love and support were, and still are, abundant.

My mom and dad--calm, kind Pete and strong, supportive Lisa--never wavered during this process of searching for and finding my birth family. I know now that they kept their concern quiet and their fear masked. Where I saw in their eyes an aloof indifference, there actually lived a deep anguish built on a foundation of protectiveness over their little girl. Typically, American families are far less demonstrative than their Colombian counterparts. During this exceptionally emotional time, the lack of transparency caused a rift, however slight, between us. And since, as I previously confessed, my head was in a cloud of genetic discovery, I failed to consider how this journey had affected my parents.

During one of my long video calls with my birth mother, translated by Juan, my dad passed behind me. María's face lit up. "Ask your parents to come to the computer," she said. "I want to meet them!" I asked her to wait for just a moment while I approached my dad, who was by then in the kitchen. "María wants to meet you," I said. To my dismay, my dad said no. I would later learn that mom and dad were hoping for a more formal introduction to María, since after all, she is the woman who gave birth to their daughter. I walked back to the computer. "Are your parents going to come and say hello?" María asked. With clammy hands and hot cheeks, I explained that they were caught off guard. I could sense my parents were uncomfortable with being put on the spot. The tension was palpable, and soon I was overcome with a slight desperation. It was the first time I became aware of the yet-unveiled dynamic between my birth family and my lifelong family. I just hoped my parents and birth mother would get along, at the very least for my sake.

* * *

I did my best to continue living as normal, although I wasn't quite sure what "normal" meant anymore. Still, I managed to complete junior college, live with my parents, spend time with friends and maintain my usual activities.

Between this "status quo," I was doing everything I could to earn enough money to afford a round-trip flight to Bogotá.

My all-consuming focus on visiting Colombia only intensified when Santiago urged me to sign onto Facebook in that sneaky kind of way that smells of surprise. When I logged on, he video-called me, and lo and behold, two new faces stared back at me: my aunt Cristina and my grandmother (abuela). María had finally told the rest of the family about me. Seeing these smiling faces--who all shared my genes--sent me soaring. Tía Cristina and my abuela began crying the moment they saw me. Emotion overwhelmed me at the sight of their reactions to me, and for the first time since finding María, I found myself near the point of tears.

"We love you so much. We wish we would have known about you," said Tía Cristina between breaths. Through my conversation with them, I learned that María had kept my existence a secret from nearly every single person in her life. "We always sensed there was something wrong or that she was hiding something. Now, it all makes sense," said my abuela, who I was told to call *Nonita*, which is a nickname for "grandma" used in the Santander region of Colombia. My head spun with this influx of information while my heart overflowed with joy.

A young man with a backpack then sat down next to my aunt and *Nonita*. He pulled out an orange and began peeling it as he yelled, "I thought I'd seen everything in life, but I never expected this s***!" This forward fellow was introduced to me as José, *el primo loco*. I wondered what he must have had to do to earn a nickname like "the crazy cousin," although his cheeky grin and airs of mischief certainly seemed like clues.

"How many more cousins do I have?" I asked them. I had at that point met a handful, which is about the cap for many American families. Not so for massive Latino families. "20-something," was their best guess. My jaw dropped, which sent them into a fit of laughter. Tía Cristina then woke up her youngest son, Felipe, and put the webcam in his face so we could meet each other. I started laughing as he wiped his eyes and muttered some half-intelligible words, clearly still too groggy to understand what was going on.

* * *

One day, I received a video message request from María, my *Nonita*, Santiago, Sara, two aunts, one uncle, and three cousins. My parents were out of town and I was home alone. Without anyone to help translate, I set out to speak with my birth family on my own--and in Spanish. A frustrating and slightly overwhelming hour of broken Spanish ensued, but I was determined to connect with my budding new family, especially since the next day was Mother's Day. This was the first Mother's Day I would be able to extend my gratitude to *both* my mom and birth mother, and now I could add to the list a *nonita* and several *tias* (aunts). Every day seemed to bring with it a mind-bending milestone.

While I spoke with my birth family, my ex-boyfriend came over to collect his belongings. He lingered as I spoke with them on the webcam, mesmerized by our interactions. His slack-jawed expression made me realize how natural this extraordinary (and by some accounts unnatural) situation had come to feel to me.

When my ex finally left, a deep sense of loneliness consumed me. I had not felt anything like this before. I thought about losing his companionship. I thought about the way the members of my birth family shared such a comfortable closeness with one another. The kind of closeness that only a lifelong bond can give you. And there I was, home alone on the other side of the screen, on the other side of the world, on the other side of an intimate relationship. Removed. Isolated. I unhinged that night and hugged my knees into my chest as my tears cradled me to sleep. I now see the rite of passage that was that night. That lonely desperation ushered me from the joyful shock of finding María into a spectrum of mixed feelings that I am only just beginning to understand.

The next morning as I got out of bed, eyes puffy and crusted, I opened Facebook to find several friend requests from even more of my Colombian cousins. After accepting each one, a slew of messages in Spanish bombarded me.

"I'm so happy to meet you!"

"Welcome to the family!"

"What's it like living in the U.S.?"

"Are you coming to visit us soon?"

Two cousins video-called me at the same time. I had no makeup on, I needed to get ready for work, and I felt emotionally and physically exhausted. And as if that weren't enough, I had no patience for trying to communicate with them in Spanish. I declined their video requests and told them I would talk to them later. I would have normally been thrilled to feel so warmly welcomed by new family members, but instead I felt myself being pulled in a million directions.

I made my way to work--a small restaurant where I waited tables. Having my birth mother now in my life, this was supposed to be my most monumental Mother's Day, and here I was, working instead of celebrating my two beautiful mothers. Grief consumed me as images flashed in my mind about my birth family, my now-broken relationship, and my mom with whom I could not spend the day. I felt like I was carrying my heart around like a stack of heavy plates, except that I didn't have the option of offloading this burden onto someone else's table. I called Juan and asked him to call María to wish her a Happy Mother's Day on my behalf. "Please tell her that I love her," I implored. Sensing the pain in my voice, Juan kindly obliged.

When I got off work, I met my American family at a restaurant to celebrate my mom. Everyone shared stories of their weeks and reminisced about childhood memories. I remained mostly silent, overcome by a rush of sentiments I couldn't quite understand, let alone explain. Everything about the moment felt uncomfortable, almost unbearable. I asked to be excused from the table and told my family I would meet them at home.

Juan called to invite me over, so I changed my clothes when I got home and grabbed my mother's gift from my night table as I headed downstairs. Before I could reach the stairs, I heard my mom's voice behind me. I guess they had left the restaurant soon after me. "Mari, can I talk to you for a minute?" she signaled for me to follow her back into my room, where she sat on my bed. "What's going on, sweetheart? Why were you so quiet during dinner?" Tears instantly began marching down my cheeks. "I feel miserable. I don't know what's come over me, but I just feel alone and tired and confused about everything. I feel like I've missed out on so much. Like I don't belong," like a crack in a dam, my angst busted forth without restraint.

"Oh, Mari, you'll be OK," she said, gently wiping the tears away. Her voice softened as she held me tight. "Why didn't you tell me any of this sooner? What you're going through is a lot to process. I'm sure you don't even know what you're feeling most of the time, and that can be confusing and exasperating," she said. My breath immediately slowed, as did the flow of tears. My mother knows how to calm anxiety and soothe worry like only a schoolteacher does. Years of practice with young minds have made her a master of empathy and diffusion. "Try not to take responsibility for everyone else's feelings," she advised. "Focus instead on yourself. Allow yourself to feel whichever emotions naturally arise. We all know you love us. You don't have to work so hard to prove it. And remember, your dad, your brothers and I, we're always here to be your backbone when you need support. We'll always be your rock, no matter what." It's as if her words went straight into my bloodstream to provide an instant dose of relief. We held each other quietly for a long while. "Thank you for being my mom," I said, finally breaking the silence.

* * *

The next day, María video called me, but Juan hadn't yet arrived at my house to help translate the conversation. I feared that without him, María and I would drown in awkward pauses. I attempted talking to her in Spanish for as long as I could, using the time to tell her about my recent breakup. Then, it dawned on me: this woman never got a chance to see her baby girl grow up. I excitedly said *"Un momento"* ("One moment"), while I jetted away to find my baby albums. One by one, I held up as many pictures of my childhood as I could find. With each baby picture, she exclaimed.

"¡Ay Dios mio, mami!" ("Oh My God, mami!")

"Que hermosa!" ("How beautiful!")

"Mira esa bebe tan feliz!" ("Look at that happy baby!")

Her eyes watered and her smile reached new heights.

My mom had apparently heard the screams of excitement followed by coos of adoration, and knew just what to do. She came upstairs and handed me more photos to show María. Still, she wasn't ready to meet my birth mother, so she stayed out of the camera's watchful eye. "Who are you with?" María asked, clearly having noticed some movement. A white lie snaked its way out of my mouth as I told her that my mom was in her room downstairs, probably resting.

My fear was that María was beginning to think my parents didn't want to talk to her. To my surprise, about 15 minutes after Juan arrived and began translating, my mom came upstairs with a piece of paper. "Will you please translate this to María for me, Juan?" she asked. I got up from my computer chair quietly and offered it to her. She sat down. Facing each other for the first time since I found María months before, they both began to weep. As did Juan. Of course, my emotionless self stood awkwardly in the background like a blank-faced statue. I wish I could have cried. *What is wrong with me?* I wondered.

My mom told María that she was always open with me about my adoption. "Tell her that I'm happy that she can be a part of Mariela's life. Tell her I hope we can also benefit from being in each other's lives," she said to Juan while looking into my birth mother's eyes. María took a deep breath, and Juan recited her response: "She's afraid you'll become jealous and think she's trying to take Mariela from you."

I couldn't believe what I was witnessing. My palms were sweating, both from excitement and anxiety. I hadn't realized until that moment just how important it was to me that they get along.

"That's absolutely not the case. Tell her there's plenty of love to be shared," my mom assured her.

"I know you have more of a right to her than me," said María.

"No one has a 'right' to me!" I finally chimed in. We all laughed.

"Tell her Pete is out of town. If he were here, I'm sure he would have said hello."

Juan translated, "María says she would like to talk to him soon because she has a lot to thank him for, also. She says she couldn't have asked for a better family for Mariela. She is eternally grateful to you for giving Mari so much love and so many opportunities in life. She is especially grateful to you for giving her a great education." My mom nodded as tears streamed down her smiling face.

After my moms said their goodbyes, I told María I loved her. *"Yo también"* (I love you too), she replied. My heart tingled.

I logged onto Facebook the following afternoon and was able to chat with my Tía Natalia for the first time. As always, I used an online translator to help move the conversation along. "I love you so much, Mariela! I had no idea you existed, but now that I do, I am so happy to know you." She went on to tell me that she had been thinking about me nonstop since learning the story of my adoption. Then, she told me she had to go to her job where she teaches young kids. I lit up as I realized we shared a common career. I told her about my Associate Degree in Early Childhood Education and about my mom's job as a first-grade teacher. I spent the rest of the day ruminating on this connection, and how grateful I felt to be so loved and accepted by my recently discovered bloodline.

* * *

Over the next few months my birth family and I continued chatting, although less frequently. My suburban Atlanta life carried on as I formulated more ways to earn money for my travels to Colombia. I asked for my friends' and family's support by setting up a donation page online titled "Send Mari to Colombia." I even resorted to selling off old possessions that no longer served me. I also pulled out my old high school Spanish books to brush up on the language. During this time, I was in the process of moving away from my parent's home to an apartment in Valdosta, Georgia, a small college town where I was studying to become a sign language interpreter. I was excited for this new chapter, but my mind was still cluttered by near-constant thoughts about my birth family. Every once in a while, I would receive a new friend request from cousins in Colombia. I had long ago lost track of exactly how many Colombian cousins I now knew. Meanwhile, I'd started dating someone new. Life was the same, but it felt different. Or maybe it was different but felt the same. I couldn't put my finger on the changes happening within me, but it felt exciting. It felt chaotic.

And then, it *finally* happened. After all the working and saving and asking for support, I bought my ticket to Bogotá.

And as if jumping through a wormhole, the day had finally come to meet this new family I'd spent months connecting with across screens and through phone receivers. Bags packed, I headed to the airport for my first trip abroad. My first time in South America. My first visit to Colombia. The first time meeting my blood relatives face to face.

My whole body pulsed. I didn't know what to expect. *Maybe I should just cancel the trip,* my irrational mind suggested. *Nice try. Bogotá, here I come.*

CHAPTER THREE
Visiting

Here I go. No turning back now, said the little cheerleader in my head. As the plane prepared to land, my heart pounded out a drum solo. It felt like my body was playing heavy metal in my chest. I landed in Bogotá, Colombia, at 9:37 p.m. on a crisp December night. I trembled with anticipation. The moment I stepped off the plane, my life would change forever (yet again).

I was traveling alone to go to Colombia to meet my birth family for the first time ever. It felt surreal. I always knew I was adopted. I thought about my birth mother--who she was, what she looked like, what her life was like--since I was a child. I fantasized about meeting her throughout my life. Oftentimes before I found her, I would see a woman who looked Latina and wonder if, by some one-in-a-million chance, she was my birth mother. I knew this was likely impossible since I was adopted from another continent, but my inner child never let go of the hope that I might miraculously run into her. In my mind's fantastical world, I would be serving myself chocolate frozen yogurt at the local froyo shop and she would walk up next to me to serve herself vanilla. I'd turn, and we'd catch each other's eyes. And instantly, we'd recognize each other. Needless to say, that's not quite the fantasy that became a reality. My reality may have been far less romantic, but it was certainly more fulfilling. And best of all, it was real.

Life seemed to crawl in slow motion the moment I stepped foot off the plane. While it frustrated me at the time, I now see the long and winding journey through the airport gave me time to emotionally prepare for the overwhelming moments to come.

I made my way through the eternal customs line. When I arrived at the kiosk 45 minutes later, the Spanish-speaking customs official asked to see my Colombian passport. Thankfully, prior to my trip a fellow Colombian adoptee suggested I bring a letter written in Spanish explaining the purpose for my visit and why I didn't know the language. And so, I was able to hand that piece of paper to the official and get through customs without an issue. I arrived at baggage claim a short walk later. It was a sprawling warehouse-sized room flanked on the left by floor to ceiling windows.

Walking over to my flight's assigned baggage carousel, a young man caught my eye through the glass to my left. There he was, my biological brother, Santiago, waving frantically. My eyes then moved from Santi to the massive group of people surrounding him. At least thirty people smiled, waved and wiped tears from their eyes. I saw my birth mother carrying Sara in her arms. I wish I could have crashed through the glass to hug them in that moment. Instead, I simply walked up to the window and began to cry. And then they began to cry. I wiped the tears in order to take in the whole scene. They had prepared signs for me handwritten in broken English that said:

"God bless each one beautiful moment we shore with you. This is your home. Your family loves you too much <3"

"Mariela welcome to Colombia your contrie. We are happy to see you."

I put my hands against the glass, and María, Sara and *Nonita* met them with their own. We cried until Santiago signaled for me to grab my other bag from the baggage claim carousel so we could bypass the barrier.

As I stood near the baggage carousel, for a moment, I understood how zoo animals must feel with so many eyes watching your every move from the other side of a glass enclosure. It was overwhelming. Then it hit me, the language barrier was going to rear its ugly head the moment I met my family outside of this room.

I realized my lip-reading instincts kicked in when I first approached the glass. That clearly did my English-thinking brain no good since I was reading Spanish-speaking lips. From zoo animal to fish out of water. This was going to be interesting.

I must have glanced up to wave at my birth family through the windows at least five times while I waited anxiously for my remaining luggage. I began to feel a little awkward--uncomfortable, even. *I hope I'm not a disappointment to them.* Finally, I grabbed my suitcase and headed toward the window hoping my biological family could show me where to go next. They spoke and signaled as terror washed over me. For the first time, I experienced the horror of incomprehension. Pushing my fears aside, they managed to guide me to the exit using hand signals and by pointing at a line of people on the other side of the large room. I joined the line and waited another 10 minutes or so until I was on the other side of the doors that would soon open to reveal my biological family. I braced myself. *Here it goes. No turning back now.* The automatic sliding doors opened, and I walked toward my family.

* * *

With a sleeping Sara wrapped around him, Santiago barreled toward me the moment I walked into the public area of the airport. I hugged him (and Sara, by association). My left arm unlocked to make way for María as she approached. How can I possibly explain the magnitude of emotions that washed over me as the four of us lingered in our embrace for minutes on end. For the first time in my life, I was touching people who shared my blood. For the first time in her life, María was holding all three of her children. It felt as if the Earth had stopped spinning just for us.

Two of my cousins carried my luggage as my big Colombian family and I headed toward the cars, taking plenty of stops for hugs and pictures along the way. We caravanned to my Tía Cristina's house, where I would be staying for the next two weeks. Metal bars covered the two-story house and every house in the vicinity. My naivete got the best of me, and so I asked, "What are the bars for?" "*Seguridad*," Santiago replied. Security. The bars are there to prevent break-ins. Uneasiness crept in with the realization that this neighborhood was far from the coziness and safety I was accustomed to in the suburbs of Atlanta. *I'm not in Kansas anymore, Toto.*

Inside the house, the festival of photos continued. My uncle handed me a shot of whiskey--Colombians are nothing if not gracious hosts. I pinched my nose and swung the brown liquor back, cringing and coughing as it stung its way down my throat. I asked Tía Cristina for a bottle of water. My friends and family in the U.S. had advised me to stay far away from the tap water in Colombia, cautioning that my American gut might not take too kindly to foreign bacteria. Judging by the curious looks on my birth family's faces when I explained this, I began to doubt the accuracy of my American friends' well-meaning counsel.

Nonita then shuffled to the kitchen where she cooked up a rice bowl topped with chicken and small boiled eggs. "I'm not very hungry, *Nonita*. Would you mind if I saved this for later?" I asked after sampling a few bites. In reality, I was on edge from an anxious day riddled with a million intense emotions, and those tiny eggs didn't do much in the way of comfort. *What kind of bird makes eggs this small?* I had never seen anyone boil an egg from anything other than a chicken before. After my abbreviated supper, most of the family lined up for a procession of hugs and cheek kisses before returning to their respective homes. Tía Cristina then showed me to my room. My cousin Felipe was kind enough to lend me his room for the entirety of my visit. I felt relieved to have a private space to rest and process my feelings after each day's end.

Speaking of rest, it was nearly impossible to shut the buzzing thoughts off that night. And anyhow, I needed to use the bathroom and had a horrible phobia of going to the restroom in the vicinity of others. I waited for my family to go to bed before sneaking over to the toilet. I had already anticipated that using the bathroom would be a challenge while visiting Bogotá. I was aware that it's common in Colombia to dispose of used toilet paper in a small trash can next to the toilet, rather than flushing it. Frankly, I was dreading my first experience. I left the bathroom that night disappointed and bloated. I was clearly feeling the effects of this roller-coaster experience from head to toe. Thankfully, my

Colombian friends Juan (my pseudo-translator) and Marco video called me that night, which was a welcome distraction from the physical discomfort of not being able to use the restroom. Juan and Marco asked me a ton of questions about my new family and told me how equally happy and jealous they felt about my getting to visit our shared motherland. Their support breathed new life into me during a time when I felt consumed by a stew of thoughts and feelings I had not even begun to process. As if cradled by a lullaby, I fell fast asleep after sharing this call with my buddies back home.

The clock hadn't yet struck 7 a.m. when my deep sleep was interrupted by surround-sound footsteps. I managed to slip back into slumber for a few minutes before the family's pet parrot screeched incessantly from its cage on the back terrace. *Was this thing being pummeled by a train?* As if reading my mind, the parrot then changed its tune, switching from that god-awful screech to a 90-minute whistling solo. Sleep was no longer on the morning's itinerary, apparently. My plan had been to go to the bathroom in the morning when everybody left for work. From the sound of all of the footsteps stomping in and out of rooms, privacy didn't seem to be an option I could count on anytime soon.

I ambled downstairs, half asleep and bloated, to find María, Sara, *Nonita*, *Nonita*'s sister and Tía Marcela waiting for me. They offered me breakfast, but I couldn't fathom squeezing anything else into my system. "Would you like to take a shower before eating?" asked María. I nodded, and off she went to fetch me a bucket of scalding water. In response to my puzzled look, my birth mother explained that many of the houses in this neighborhood don't have a limitless supply of hot running water, so a bucket of boiled water makes it possible to greet the day with a warm shower. I grabbed the bucket and thanked them for the lovely gesture. I washed myself, was able to finally use the bathroom, and was less disturbed than I thought I would have been at the inability to flush the toilet paper. I got dressed and joined my family downstairs for breakfast. The six of us took turns eating since the table only seated four people.

My first full day in Bogotá sent my groggy senses into overdrive.

Delicious food, a wide-eyed car ride, polluted streets, stunning mountain vistas, bustling shopping centers and packed city sidewalks kept me on high alert without pause. Vincente's taxi facilitated the aforementioned car ride, which was my first introduction to a sunlit Bogotá. In this South American capital city, people interpret traffic laws as mere suggestion. Driving in that city is a true test of courage. Colombian drivers could all be related to champion racer Juan Pablo Montoya with how expertly they weave in and out of cars, dodge obstacles and screech to a halt inches before you think it's too late. Lanes practically don't exist, despite being painted onto the road (nice try, city officials). Cyclists squeeze between the cars daringly on cluttered roads. It's a free-for-all. And yet, I don't recall seeing any accidents. I wondered how many traffic laws I had just seen violated had U.S. rules applied in Colombia. And while we're on the subject, how is it that U.S. drivers seem to have so many more accidents despite having such strict traffic governance? Counterintuitive, to say the least.

Vincente pulled up at the shopping center where many of my biological family members work, and I rushed out thanking the heavens to have made it in one piece. María, Sara, Tías Cristina and Marcela, Felipe, and Vincente shuffled out after me. They led me through the maze of tiny *tiendas* (stores) selling shirts and jeans and shoes and jewelry and purses and perfumes and kitchen tools and bed sheets and so much more to the shop Tío (uncle) Pepe and Tía Cristina own. Santiago and my cousin Antonio were already there staffing our family's *tienda*.

Each tiny shop is at most 16 square feet. Shelves line every inch of the walls, and in my family's case, sneakers dominate those shelves. The *tiendas* offer enough room for one chair to be placed in the middle from which the shop attendant can greet customers. With each passerby, attendants call after them by saying, *"A la orden,"* which translates roughly to "At your service." Walking through these malls, or *centros*, can be an overwhelming experience as a near endless echo of *"a la orden"* follows you without reprieve.

I spent the next several hours at the shoe store with Santiago, Antonio and Felipe on the top floor of this four-story *centro*. Santiago and I eventually walked to a restaurant down the road to meet up with María, my aunts, my cousin Patricia, and Sara. I sat in the restaurant and looked around, taking in every detail of my surroundings. It was hard to believe I was in Bogotá, Colombia, being immersed in my birth family's day-to-day life. My brain felt divided between the comfortable, sheltered life I had known in Alpharetta, Georgia, and this incomprehensibly different society, way of life, and culture. Somehow, Alpharetta seemed so...irrelevant. Eventually, Santiago and I walked back to the *tienda*, where he introduced me to an English-speaking friend named Andrés, who generously walked me to a nearby store where I bought minutes for the ramshackle old phone my friend had lent me for the trip.

Finally--only after the most frightening car ride of my life--I was back in the safety and comfort of Tía Cristina's house. After a delicious dinner of the traditional *bandeja paisa* (a platter of food consisting of beans, rice, chicharron, steak, fried egg, avocado, fried plantains and an arepa), Tía Cristina called me over to the living room with a chipper *"Mari!"* The way she pronounced the *r* in "Mari" made it sound like a new name. We sat down on the sofa and she began showing me childhood pictures of her sons and my other cousins. I glanced at one picture across the table. She smirked, catching my lingering stare, and brought it forward. "These are all of your *primos* (cousins) standing in a line from youngest to oldest," she said nostalgically. "You would have been standing...there!" she exclaimed while rubbing my back gently. I yearned to be in that picture. And though I tried not to overthink it, the gut-wrenching feeling of exclusion rose slowly, involuntarily, into my throat.

* * *

The following day hit me like a whirlwind. "Time to get up, Mari!" hollered the little voice peeking through the door. The voice belonged to my Tía Marcela and was soon joined by a second, lower-pitched tone, this time from Tía Natalia, who had taken the bull by the horns and charged straight into the room to get me moving. I had no idea I was going to meet Tía Natalia today, let alone in that state. Then again, I was often unaware of the many things that happened around me during my visit. I kept hearing the word *vestido* until my half-asleep brain fully awoke to realize they were telling me we had to go find Sara a *dress*. Apparently, Tía Natalia's son Juanes (short for Juan Esteban) was getting married the following week and was in Bogotá for the weekend to take care of some final wedding arrangements. Toothbrush. Bathroom time. Pot of boiling water. *Empanada* (popular Colombian snack consisting of a fried corn flour shell that is typically stuffed with meat). I sped through my morning routine as Tía Natalia readied Sara. Gabriela, the bride to be, arrived during all of the chaos, and soon thereafter we were shuffling out the door and into the taxi waiting outside.

Our first stop was to get my little sister's dress. Sara tried it on in the store and ran around dancing in it like a little princess. I took lots of videos and pictures to capture the moment. With Sara's dress in hand, it was time to pick up Gabriela's wedding dress. While waiting for our next cab, my rosy-eyed wedding glasses were stripped from me as I noticed the magnitude of suffering that surrounded us. Poverty like I'd never seen came into view. People without shoes. Without legs, even. One legless man crawled on the ground just a few yards from us. I could feel his desperation, his long-deceased dignity. I wanted to help him, to comfort his pain and ease what I imagined was an unbearable sense of loss. I looked around, expecting to see those around me experiencing the same hurt for this fellow human. But I saw nothing of the sort. In fact, I wondered if I was the only one who could see this poor soul crawling on the sidewalk. Every face was turned away from him. *Do they not care?* I wondered with a heavy heart. Or, perhaps even more heartbreaking, *are these people so used to seeing this level of poverty in the streets that it no longer phases them? Would I, too, one day become numb to this kind of suffering?* I continued to question everything even further. *How much of the rest of the world is like this? Is this reality?* My mind raced as we climbed into the taxi and left the man behind.

The day carried on full of errands and visits and food. After dinner, we walked to a salon where María met us. She paid for me to get my hair washed and styled, and my makeup done. I told her how grateful I was for her generosity. Sara was going to get her nails done. She sat down in the chair and stared at the nail technician, who was across the room talking to her coworker. Sara's stare turned into a glare as she tapped her small fingers on her chair and yelled, *¡Estoy esperando!* ("I'm waiting!"). I erupted in laughter--this confident little lady always seems to exclaim what others are thinking but are too prudent to say.

I often see myself in Sara--the way she thinks, how she radiates joy, her high-energy antics and femininity. I hope we are close as she grows up. I hope I make a lasting impact on her. I hope I'm not just a passing phase in her life.

* * *

After the salon, Santi and my three cousins took me to El Centro Comercial Calima, a sprawling mall where we met two fellow adoptees. Monica was an adoptee from Minnesota who had moved to Bogotá a year before to be with her boyfriend. She had already met her birth family and navigated a similar journey of self- and cultural discovery. Josh, a fellow

AFC group member from New Jersey, was in Bogotá visiting his birth family.

"I'm jealous you get to stay for so much longer," Josh said. I was able to catch him on the last night of his visit, and his yearning signaled something within me. As adoptees, all of our stories are so vastly different and yet so remarkably similar. For many of us, our native lands seem to pull at us like giant magnets. I had already noticed a tiny spark of attachment within myself--one that I knew would soon turn into a glowing flame.

I felt at home with my little trio of adoptees. Josh picked on me playfully for my broken Spanglish. "That's how I sounded when I first visited Colombia to meet my family," he said.

"God, it feels good to finally speak English with someone!" I laughed. I missed being able to express myself fluidly and authentically. For the first time during my stay, I was able to speak in my native language with people who understand my cultural mannerisms and norms. I was also thrilled to have Santiago, Antonio and Felipe there to hear me as my authentic self, expressing myself so naturally in English to my new friends.

I often wonder if my personality is distorted by the language barrier. I'm not able to fully express myself to my birth family because we lack the ability to have deep verbal conversations, so how could they get an accurate sense of who I am? And vice versa, for that matter.

Beyond the initial culture shock of arriving in Colombia, I experienced a steady increase in glaring instances of cultural disparities between the culture that raised me and that which created me. During one instance at the mall with Monica and Josh, the group sat down to eat burgers and fries at a popular fast-food chain called El Corral. As my cousins and I began to feel full, I got up to throw out the rest of my food while they continued chomping at their burgers. Everyone at the table jumped up when they saw me walking toward the trash. "Don't throw your food away!" called Santi. "We don't waste food when there are starving people on the streets," explained Antonio.

"But I'm full," I said, my head hanging low and my belly about to burst.

Antonio began cutting up the burger while he explained that the family was once extremely poor, and how that experience instilled in them a respect and appreciation for *having*. They split up my burger between the three of them and helped me finish it.

* * *

As we left the mall, our time with Monica and Josh now behind us, my brother turned and asked when I planned to return to Bogotá. "As soon as I make enough money," I told him. I was met with nothing but silence as Santi and my cousins looked straight ahead. "I want to visit as often as I can," I reassured them.

If you had described Bogotá to me before my visit--detailing the poverty and pollution, telling me about throwing used toilet paper in the garbage instead of flushing it, and taking showers with pots of boiling water--my reaction would have been to run the opposite way. I was raised in the northern suburbs of Atlanta, Georgia, where I enjoyed a simple, privileged life. Sure, I have endured my own set of trials, but I don't know what it's like to fight for my survival or to have my basic needs go unmet. I now see that much of my life has been luxurious in comparison to the extreme obstacles so many people in this world face every day of their lives. I can't help but to feel spoiled by my middle-class American upbringing.

Because there are no guarantees in the life of a lower- or even middle-class Colombian, in this country the hustle is *real*. Americans may well be hustlers, but money-making tactics are vastly different than in this in-your-face Colombian lifestyle. In Bogotá, salespeople take to the streets to sling their goods and services inches from a passerby's face. They chum the waters then cast their nets to reel in the day's catch. Americans, on the other hand, mostly take a subtle approach nuanced by marketing strategies and psychological innuendo that's meant to subconsciously compel you to buy what they're selling. That's a waste of time to most Colombian entrepreneurs. They have no interest in coaxing or courting. Either you want the product or not.

Bogotános (people from Bogotá) are especially persistent and energetic. I studied them with each trip we took through the city, intent on understanding the city's frantic energy. It seems people here have to work doubly as hard as middle-class Americans just to earn enough food for the day. This do-what-it-takes mindset lives in me, too. I experienced it as soon as I set my mind to visiting Bogotá. Finding revenue streams wherever I could helped me afford the flight that led to the life-changing experience of meeting my birth family face-to-face. In that *small* sense, I can understand the pride that comes from buying something earned through hard work.

Perhaps the most beautiful thing about *Bogotános*, hustlers as they are, is their unstoppable joy regardless of how hard they have to work to get the little they have. No one complains or plays victim of circumstance; instead, they enjoy the lives they work so hard to build.

"I promise I'll visit again soon," I reiterated to Santiago. Little did he know, Colombia was stealing my heart.

* * *

Cultural differences between the U.S. and Colombia go far beyond bathing methods and money-making tactics. Families function in very distinct ways in the two societies. Several members of my Colombian family work together, either at the shoe store or at restaurants. On the other hand, every member of my American family has a different career, workplace and even lifestyle. Generally speaking, an American child's goal is often to leave the nest as soon as they graduate from high school. American nuclear families are raised together, then they move away to live separate lives, often in other states or countries. In Colombia, sticking together as a family means living and working with one another throughout a lifetime. Could these deep family bonds be the reason Colombians seem happier?

CHAPTER FOUR
Discovering

With each passing day, the roots of my family tree began to unfold. During one quiet afternoon in my aunt's house, my cousin Antonio translated as Tía Natalia told me about how *Nonito* (my grandfather) left *Nonita* (my grandmother) when María and her siblings were very young. The oldest of the seven kids was 14 years old, and the youngest was four months old when *Nonito* turned his back on the family. *Nonita* was left to raise the kids on her own, which she did with an open heart and resilient spirit. Unsurprisingly, *Nonita* is the beloved and respected matriarch of the family to this day, even after *Nonito* made his way back to the roost a decade later. But he didn't return because he missed his family--as Tía Natalia described it, he came back in need of medical care. He was back in everyone's lives from then on, although he certainly doesn't live with *Nonita* at Tía Cristina's house. In fact, I never did find out where he lays his head.

I met him for the first time days before I knew about him leaving my *Nonita*. Regardless of this new information I received about him, I decided to accept him for who he is now, rather than judging him based on past mistakes. He was the only person in the family that tried to communicate with me by pointing and using hand gestures rather than speaking.

Ironically, he didn't know I was working toward my bachelor's degree in sign language interpreting. Even so, it was impossible to make sense of his gestures.

Something strange was starting to happen within me. The more I learned about my new family, the more I felt like an outsider. And yet, the more time I spent with them, the more I felt a part of something greater than myself.

That greater-than-self feeling was never more present than when I spent time with Sara. Even when all I wanted was to spend the day exploring Bogotá, staying home instead to play hide and seek, watch YouTube videos and play phone games with her felt worthwhile. I would watch her, the way her mind connected dots and spun webs, the way her larger-than-life personality somehow fit inside her four-year-old frame, and it always left me beaming with pride. *This is my sister, my bloodline,* I would say to myself like a mental pinch to make sure it was real.

Sara is particularly smart for her age. She has a strong memory and is quite independent for someone who had at that point spent less than half a decade on this planet. I feel like I'm looking in a tiny mirror when I'm with her. In fact, our similarities make it hard for me to outsmart her. She seems to have an ability to read people on a deeper level, and so she always seems to be one step ahead. She carries herself like a miniature adult--with more confidence and poise than many adults I know, actually. We are both passionate people. It was a rush to witness our physical and emotional similarities unfold.

Sara was obsessed with my smartphone and never wanted to put it down. In fact, *Nonita* had even expressed concerns about her having too much screen time. Nonetheless, watching videos and playing games on technology took up a lot of our time at the house together. One afternoon, Sara and I were lying in bed watching "The Three Little Pigs" in Spanish on YouTube. My birth mom walked in and sat on the bed with us. I looked at them watch as the Big Bad Wolf huffed and puffed. My breath stopped for a moment as I realized that, for the first time in my life, I was sharing a bed with someone who came from the same womb as I did. And there, just a foot away, was the woman who birthed us both. The pigs stood their ground and managed to trick the wolf. We all laughed, filling the room with a harmony of similar noises.

Sara then begged me to take pictures with her. One blurry photo after another, she snapped away insistently. Every time I tried to take the phone back to help her take a clearer photo, she would defiantly move it out of my reach. I felt the heat of irritation rising in my spine. I was losing my patience, but I felt obligated to appease her. I didn't want to disappoint Sara, especially not in front of María (who didn't seem to mind Sara's behavior). I took a deep breath and planted a smile on my face to avoid any confrontation.

That evening, we went to my uncle's house to celebrate his mother-in-law's birthday. On the way to the party, I stuck my hand out of the window, pointing to something as we passed it. "Don't do that!" yelled everyone in unison. I yanked my arm back in, rattled by the sudden outburst. I later learned that thieves sometimes reach into a car window to grab valuables like a purse or watch. *Oops.* At the party we ate lots and had a good time. *Mi familia* (my family) laughed together about topics that my English mind struggled to understand. I did my best to follow their fast-paced conversations, but to no avail. I sat and enjoyed observing their mannerisms instead. During our time there, my uncle surprised me with a Colombian *ruana* (poncho). I thanked him for the gift and felt excited to have such an authentic souvenir. Before we left, my Tía Cristina wrapped up some cake to bring back for the family members who didn't come with us to the party. I thought that was kind of her, and wished it was more common in American culture to do the same. On our way back from the party, we dropped Santi off where he lives...María's house. It was the first time I got to see my birth mom's home, although only from the outside for a fleeting moment. More metal security bars were all I could gather.

After returning to Tía Cristina's house, I sped upstairs to decompress on my own. I'm not used to being around so many people day in and day out, and especially not living under the same roof as those people. This near-constant level of interaction left me feeling drained and in desperate need of alone time by sunset. The culture of independence in the U.S. offers me ample space for time alone in my day-to-day life. And yet, with the lack of privacy I came to appreciate how rarely I felt lonely while I was with my Colombian family.

* * *

The sun felt particularly bright the next morning as it cascaded through the windows and filled each room with its golden warmth. My morning routine was fueled by an energized anticipation that landed me at the breakfast table in less time than usual. I was less than a week into my visit and my best friend was about to arrive in Bogotá from Medellín. I met Kurt in the AFC Facebook group. He's a Colombian adoptee who also found and reconnected with his birth family. He lives in Miami, Florida, and grew up in Seattle, Washington. He never identified with the predominately white society in Seattle and, as a result, moved to South Beach, the land of Latin culture, palm trees, Brazilian bikinis, and hurricanes. I was ecstatic when we realized we were crossing paths during our respective visits to Colombia. Despite having met in person only twice, we shared a deep bond fortified by late-night Skype calls, commiserations about adoption, and our mutually outspoken ways. Few people made me laugh and feel understood like Kurt. And nothing made me more excited than the idea of spending time in Bogotá with someone who knew the real, uncensored Mari. Kurt is what Colombians call a *parcero* or *parce*, a real friend. Having a close *parce* who lived through similar experiences as I did--being adopted from Colombia, growing up in a white family in the U.S., living in predominantly white towns--and who also expresses themselves in the same (fun-loving and boisterous) way that I do has become an essential part of my personal growth. Kurt inspires me to be the best version of myself, and he does so with a level of understanding of which not many people are capable. What's more, before I was able to visit Bogotá myself, Kurt was my best source of insight into the inner workings of Colombian culture, since by then Colombia had become his second home. Suffice it to say, I'm grateful for his friendship.

A car blared its horn just outside the house as I scarfed down the last bite of my cheese *arepa con queso*. I leapt up, ripped my jacket from the coat hook and flew out of the door, yelling for Felipe as I beelined for Vincente's taxi. Felipe climbed into the back, and soon the faithful cab was spitting out fumes as it chugged along to the bus station where Kurt was scheduled to arrive. I screamed the moment I saw Kurt amble out of his bus. *"Parcero!"* I leapt toward him and wrapped my arms around his broad shoulders. He grunted while I clung onto him. His eyes rolled while a hint of a smile peeked through his fake distaste for my over-the-top affection. As if triggered by a starter pistol, Kurt and I began spouting off updates, interrupted only by polite introductions between he, Felipe and Vincente.

"Get ready," I said as we pulled up to Tía Cristina's house.

"I know the drill," said Kurt, who understood that he was about to enter the front lines where an army of hugs and kisses and an artillery of questions were undoubtedly already in formation. It's the Colombian way.

Kiss after hug after question, Kurt maneuvered through the onslaught of greetings like a champion. We finally found ourselves crammed elbow to elbow at the kitchen table eating the *pan con queso* (bread with cheese) Tía Marcela had prepared for us. After a few minutes of conversation in the kitchen, I suggested we take a walk through the neighborhood.

The things I see play out on the streets of Bogotá never cease to amaze me. On my walk with Kurt, I finally had with me someone who understood how bizarre those moments are to a foreigner. On the first block, we saw a man sweeping the grass with a broom. Not 100 feet away, a homeless man sharpened his knife on the curb. On the other side of the block, a poor soul dug through the trash for what I can only assume was food. All the while, industrious *Bogotános* tried to beckon us by shouting promises of can't-miss-out, gotta-have-it gum or fruit or bracelets or figurines. The next block featured a park with a precious, albeit weathered, nativity scene in honor of the forthcoming Christmas holiday. I pulled my phone out of my back pocket and tapped the camera icon as we walked toward the scene. A mangy dog was fast asleep in front of the tattered statue of Joseph as flies swarmed his vacuum-sealed rib cage. Two dogs with matted fur snored deeply just a few feet away. I had never seen so many homeless dogs as I did during my time in Bogotá. I later tried to explain to my American friends that crossing paths with stray dogs in Bogotá is like seeing squirrels in Georgia--they're practically a part of the natural landscape to locals. Bogotános are so accustomed to stray dogs wandering about that they seem blind to them. I assume that most people in Bogotá are so focused on feeding their families each day, that they have neither the time nor the money to care for an animal--which is just another warm body to nourish. Pets (and the ability to care for them) took on new meaning for me after I witnessed so many homeless cats and dogs in Bogotá.

Later that day, Kurt, Felipe, Tío Pepe and I went to my family's shoe store. *Nonita* had prepared lunch for Santi, Tía Cristina and my cousin Antonio, and it was Tío Pepe's job to deliver the goods. With all the lunches handed out and devoured, Kurt and I found ourselves sitting in a corner of the *centro* watching my cousins climb up and down three flights of stairs to fetch shoe styles, organize boxes and replenish inventory. Up the stairs they would jet, rushing down a few minutes later clutching the twine that held a stack of boxes together for maximum efficiency. The mall was abuzz with sprightly teens leaping up and down the stairs as their middle-aged counterparts attended to customers on the ground floor in the fight for their small slice of the commercial pie.

Later on, as Kurt and I chatted with Antonio about the business, we found out that most of the shoes sold in the *centro* were Chinese knockoffs. I was impressed by the quality of the replicas. Tía Cristina recounted how just a few days prior the police had dropped in on the vendors and threatened to bust them for selling counterfeit goods. I remembered exactly which day she was referencing--that was the first time my family took me to the store. I had seen dozens of police officers weaving through the *centro* and its many miniature shops. *This place has some tight security,* I thought at the time. "Why wasn't anyone arrested?" I asked Tía Cristina. She rubbed her thumb and index finger together, and I immediately understood. For what I'm sure is no small price, the vendors are able to continue earning their daily bread by selling those pristine knockoffs. And that's how I learned about the widespread corruption in Bogotá's police force.

Kurt and I kept watching the well-oiled machine march forward with its many moving pieces and parts. A pair of pillowy hands covered my eyes, and a breathy laugh followed suit. "María?" I said. She hopped from behind me with an exuberance I had yet to witness. She had been working at my uncle's restaurant nearby and decided to pay us an impromptu visit. But this was a new version of the María with whom I had spent the past few days. This María was beaming. Cracking jokes. She seemed happy. She seemed...well, whole. Our conversations were able to move along more fluidly with Kurt serving as our translator. At one point (in between toothy grins and cheesy jokes), she asked if I liked Colombia enough to return. "Of course!" I responded.

"I want to meet your family. And I hope one day we can all feel united as one family," she said.

"I would love that!" I responded.

"Do you think your parents are afraid you'll stop loving them now that you found us?"

That was the least of my parents'--and my--concerns. No one on Earth could replace my mom and dad. I smiled and said, "They have nothing to fear. They're happy I found you. They know what this means to me."

* * *

Soon after María left, Kurt and I ventured off to walk around the neighborhood. On our walk, we saw people hawking their wares, bloodshot eyes crowning dark circles that hinted at their laborious lives. I wondered if they had ever experienced the luxury of rest. All these people--the women pushing food carts and the kids carrying baskets and the men selling from overstuffed stalls--they were such hard workers. And I had yet to catch them complaining. In this neighborhood, homeless people wandered the parks eating trash alongside crowds of police officers armed with automatic weapons and expertly trained canines. The buildings showed their age through faded paint and deep-set cracks. And yet, all of the characters move about energetically and, dare I say, happily. Their positive energy infuses their surroundings with a joyous sense of purpose that detracts from what may be perceived as disheartening.

One thing has become abundantly certain to me during this time of cultural discovery. Lower-class Colombians don't see an equal return on their hard work. They bend over backward daily in return for excruciatingly little compensation. Everywhere I look, I see wasted potential. These blue-collar workers get stuck selling on the streets in order to survive. With little to no upward mobility built into the lower-middle and lower classes, these people are resigned to a lifetime of street vending unless they risk everything to make potentially life-changing career moves. I can't imagine how they would even find time to earn a college degree without facing starvation in the process. This brings to mind some of the people I know in the U.S. who dedicate a bare minimum of effort to their jobs, and yet are able to afford luxuries like ample houses, new cars, smartphones, and lest we forget, hot water. And still, these fortunate souls find reasons to curse their all-too-comfortable lives. In watching my birth family earn their living, I witnessed a work ethic that left me feeling inspired and amazed. The painstaking efforts they put into each day serves only to keep their refrigerators stocked--still, they are left without hot showers. It feels unfortunate and unfair.

Arriving back at the shoe store, Kurt and I offered to help my brother and cousins in hopes that it would make the time pass more quickly. But after Antonio detailed their process, I knew there was no way we could perform the same tasks without inadvertently throwing off their finely tuned system of organized chaos. We would have to find another way to move the clock's hands along.

Nature was calling, so I figured I could make an adventure out of using a public restroom for the first time since arriving in Bogotá. I asked Tía Cristina where I could find the ladies' room, and she pointed the way before handing me a voucher that she instructed me to hand to the bathroom attendant. I approached the bathrooms, which had a small booth with an even smaller woman sitting inside. I handed her the voucher through the window and in exchange I received about seven squares of toilet paper folded neatly. Kurt used the restrooms before my aunt had given her Public Peeing 101 course, vouchers included, and so he found himself having to pay the 500 pesos toilet toll. Paying to go to the bathroom? Now, this left me culture shocked. I had never paid to use a restroom in the U.S. It seemed unethical to charge someone to relieve their bodily functions. Regardless, I did my best to set those preconceptions aside.

* * *

Finally, our time at the shoe store came to a close. Kurt and I made our way back to Tía Cristina's house, where Tía Natalia was waiting with snacks at the kitchen table. As we sat and talked idly with her, flowing easily thanks to Kurt's translation skills, our conversation meandered onto the topic of my birth and adoption. In the safety (and rarity) of a still house, she divulged how María shared the news of my existence with the family earlier that year. She detailed how she and most of her siblings, my *tíos* and *tías*, crumbled to tears upon learning that their niece had existed all this time, having never known her family or culture. With misty eyes, Tía Natalia seemed to be reliving those shocking moments as she recounted them. I realized the family had likely not spoken much of it since the initial earth-shattering revelation. She continued opening up, releasing with each word a treasure trove of family history. And within the goldmine of information, she unearthed the extraordinary story of how Vincente and María met.

According to Tía Natalia, María was overcome by depression after making what would be the hardest decision of her life: putting her first-born child up for adoption. She was in a state of emotional ruin, the depths of which included contemplations of suicide so as to stop the pain. One grief-stricken day, she was walking down the street when she hailed a cab. Upon sitting in its back seat, María erupted into tears. It's as if a well of pain had suddenly overflowed, leaving her drowning in that deep sadness she had been guarding from the world. The driver, distraught by his passenger's sudden breakdown, asked her what was wrong and if he could help. María had not told a single soul about the adoption and the hole it had carved in her heart. But something about this driver, something about his kindness and sincerity--and perhaps her need to share this burden with someone, anyone--compelled María to tell this well-meaning stranger every detail of her unwanted pregnancy. She told him how the baby's father pressured her to get an abortion. She told him how she hid the pregnancy from her family. And finally, she told him how she had so recently birthed and parted ways with her bright-eyed baby girl.

That driver was Vincente. That cab ride gave root to a friendship and that friendship blossomed into a marriage and that marriage gave life to my half-brother, Santiago, and my half-sister, Sara.

I don't think I breathed once while Tía Natalia told the story. I was stunned by the serendipity of it all. If María hadn't put me up for adoption, would she and Vincente have ever met? Would Santiago and Sara exist? I sat in amazement as I realized the day María put me up for adoption was like the flap of a butterfly's wings that triggered new possibilities for love and life.

During the course of the story, I also found out that Vincente was much older than my birth mom. In fact, I think he is close in age to *Nonito*, which I found quite unusual. Apparently, Vincente had a daughter, Marta, from his first marriage. Now an adult, Marta lived in Connecticut. *Nonita* mentioned Sara looks a lot more like me than she does Marta. I was glad to hear that.

* * *

In the hours that passed, we saw the house come alive with family members stopping by for a bite and a visit, coming home from work, dropping something off, and the like. The amount of energy that this quaint home holds during any given moment is astounding. As day turned into night, those who didn't live there left and those who did made their way to bed. Silence fell over the house at an unusually early hour, leaving my cousin Antonio and me by ourselves in the living room.

Antonio's English had improved during my short visit, which made conversation between us not just possible, but also enjoyable.

"The family feel guilty for work so much while you here," he told me in his broken English. He explained that they wanted me to be able to see Bogotá's sights, visit museums, and experience the beautiful landscapes. Instead, because they have to earn their daily bread and don't feel comfortable allowing me to explore on my own, I haven't done much other than memorize every corner of the house since my arrival. Other than accompanying someone to run an errand occasionally, I had been either sitting idly in the house or at the shoe store.

"The wedding will be fun!" he said reassuringly. I had forgotten that the coming weekend was my cousin Juanes' wedding. I felt a sudden glimmer of excitement as I realized my first family outing was soon to come. Seeing me perk up at the thought of having something to do, Antonio then said he would try to take me on a *chiva* before I left. *Chivas* are brightly colored buses that were once the way people got around in Ye Olde Colombia but are now party buses marketed mostly to tourists.

Antonio may have been astutely picking up on my building restlessness. I was having fun, I suppose. But an itch was starting to appear--first, over my inability to express myself easily; then, as my inability to plan my own days or venture out on my own began to wear on me. In the U.S., I have full control over what I do, where I go, with whom I spend time, and when I leave my house. The restrictions in

Bogotá, whether for my safety or because of my family's work schedule, kept me feeling like a bird with clipped wings. I couldn't even think about leaving Tía Cristina's house without an escort, as they feared for my safety in this particular neighborhood. And despite everyone's warmth, care and heartwarming generosity, I felt caged. In fact, Tía Cristina's house is enclosed on all sides by metal-fence-like bars that are close to ten feet tall. A key is needed to leave as much as it's needed to get in. It felt more like a cage with each passing day.

Regardless of my growing itch, I'll admit it was nice to feel protected by them.

CHAPTER FIVE
Comparing

One thing no one forewarned me about Colombia is the epidemic of time dyslexia taking over the country. I'm convinced when someone says, "Meet me at 12:30," a Colombian hears, "Meet me at 3:20." They brush it off as "Latino time," but I call that chronic lateness. Kurt suffers from a debilitating case of time dyslexia, something of which my American upbringing seems to have cured me. I guess Kurt's predisposition for it was unshakably strong.

On my sixth day in Bogotá, Kurt was to meet me back at Tía Cristina's house at noon. He had made plans to stay at his friend's house across town the night before. I awoke that day, meandered away some time by watching TV, and watched as the clock marched past its twelve o' clock position. No Kurt and no call. I called him, and on the other end was an out-of-breath Kurt with a background track of honking cars and unintelligible voices shouting. He was playing soccer, apparently unaware that we had agreed to meet at a specified time. Pangs of jealousy reverberated through me as I thought about Kurt enjoying the day while I remained stuck in the house yet again. *I'll make him pay,* I thought. And I did. Later that day, when Kurt finally found his way back to me while I was at the restaurant where my cousin Patricia and Tío Oscar work, I made him eat the heaps of meat I couldn't finish. "That's your punishment for making me wait for so long," I jokingly sneered as he grimaced through each bite. Finally, after all the waiting and eating and walking, it was time to go to the bus station where we would start our journey to Suba, a large locality in northwest Bogotá, to visit Kurt's birth family. We had talked for so many months about his odd family dynamic, the way tensions build then settle, how he found his birth mother and how she responded. Kurt hadn't seen his birth mother in months, and I was unbearably curious to meet the characters who shared my best friend's genes and claimed lead roles in his most dramatic tales.

Packed arm to arm, leg to leg, and practically cheek to cheek, we crammed into the bus for a rocky 45-minute ride. Body odor clung in the air like a moment frozen in time, reminding its audience of a long day spent working in the sun, cleaning on hands and knees, and frying *arepas* over a hot stove. *I can finally empathize with sardines*, I thought. My body was having none of it. A wave of nausea hit both Kurt and me and sent in reinforcements in the form of clammy hands. *All we have to do is make it through 40 minutes and then transfer to another bus*, I told myself. The second bus came to a stop just in time. We scurried off and took deep breaths, devouring every ounce of fresh oxygen our lungs could hold. A five-minute walk brought us to our final destination: the small produce market that Kurt's birth mom owns.

She was manning one of the registers when we walked in. "Hola, Kurt," she said with only a little more enthusiasm than if she'd just welcomed a regular customer. We settled into a corner of the store. There we waited, dodging customers, forcing chit chat, and staring into the distance. There we waited for Kurt's birth mom to take advantage of a lull in the line that would allow one of her many employees to take her place while she spent time with us. There we waited as the last customer in line paid for his goods, freeing her for the first time since we arrived. And there we waited as she stayed firmly planted at the register until, minutes later, the next customer approached. At least an hour passed as we stood there and waited until the air was too cold and the sun too far set for us to stay any longer.

We had told my cousins we would likely be back at Tía Cristina's house by eight o' clock that evening, at the latest. We got to the market at 6 p.m., and after an hour or more of waiting, I felt a chill of anxiety flowing up my chest and into my throat. We had to go soon, and although I understood how disappointed--and hurt--Kurt must have felt over his birth mom's disinterest, getting back to my aunt's house was the main thing on my mind. Little did I know, we still had a few more of Kurt's friends and family members to visit before embarking on the bumpy ride back to Tía Cristina's. I dug my elbow into his side and widened my eyes--the universal signal for "Let's go!" Kurt and I unglued ourselves from our designated corner and said goodbye to his birth mom. "You're leaving? So soon?" she asked him in Spanish simple enough for me to grasp. I couldn't believe what I was seeing. Her disinterest turned immediately into victimhood as she piled a heaping dose of mother's guilt onto Kurt. She asked Kurt if he was staying the night at her home, and he said he was going back with me that night. She dialed up the guilt trip in response. Kurt seemed confused. He and his birth mom had never discussed anything about him staying the night during our visit. I was in disbelief watching her try to manipulate him. In that moment, I felt grateful that María had never treated me with such selfishness. We eventually left the store to pay his cousin a visit. After arriving in a dark alley, I was unsure whether I wanted to continue on to the apartment. Kurt pointed at the decrepit stairs, and I looked at him as if he had just asked me to walk a tightrope made of snakes. He nudged me forward laughing, and up the steps I went. His cousin's apartment was small and cold and not what I would call "cozy." Her bed was crammed in a corner and the rest of the apartment was cluttered with odds and ends. There was hardly enough space to walk let alone sit and relax for a while. A few minutes later, it was time to head to Kurt's biological sister's house.

Once we got there, I rushed to the bathroom. I had been holding my bladder for several hours, having felt deterred to use the bathroom at the produce store and his cousin's house.

Both bathrooms lacked what I considered to be restroom essentials--toilet seats, lighting and toilet paper. His sister's bathroom wasn't much cleaner, but this Goldilocks had run out of options. Hands washed, I followed the sound of Kurt's voice to the room where he and his sister were talking. I froze. There, sitting on the couch, was Kurt's sister with both her breasts spilling freely from her blouse as her four-year-old child joyfully drank its milk. Kurt stared at me, his face contorted with the agony of discomfort. "Definitely one of the most awkward things I have ever experienced," he said to me in English, knowing his sister wouldn't understand. We both laughed as she glanced at us inquisitively.

The chill in the air turned into bone-rattling cold as the glow of sunset turned into the pitch blackness of night. Our last stop led us to Kurt's friend's house. A devout Catholic, Kurt's friend also happens to make her living by stripping in front of a webcam. A virtual stripper, if you will. She dances on the webcam for men who watch her from all over the world. Kurt told me that the last time he visited her, he wound up babysitting her child while she stripped in the other room. Apparently, it amply pays her bills and allows her to raise her adorable child in relative comfort. Kurt and his friend spent an hour catching up in Spanish while I sat in silence. By then, the anxiety about returning to Tía Cristina's house had fully set in. It was time to go.

We made our way back to my family, opting for the blessed comfort of a cab over the sardine-like experience of a bus. It was only a day later that I discovered FANA, my orphanage, had relocated to Suba. Apparently, I had been within walking distance of it while visiting Kurt's family.

* * *

We got back to my family's southern *barrio* (neighborhood), where my cousins awaited us on the street. The day's adventures had me dreaming of a warm night of uninterrupted sleep. Juanes' wedding was tomorrow, and that brought with it an early morning, a long road trip and a day full of dancing, eating and meeting new members of my birth family. But, alas, the best laid plans were made to be disrupted by well-meaning cousins and a half-empty bottle of *aguardiente*. *Aguardiente* is anise-flavored liqueur that has enough power to fuel Colombia's wildest nights (and probably also fuel a jet engine). Antonio, José and Santi had gathered a group of five of their friends from the *centro* to whisk Kurt and I into a night of drinking, dancing, and more drinking. I walked up to the group and a shot of *aguardiente* materialized in my hand. Reluctantly, I swallowed the clear rocket fuel in a single, searing gulp. The boys cheered and slapped my back, laughing as my face contorted into a twisted grimace. It was nice to feel a sense of camaraderie and belonging, but it was abundantly clear I would not be able to match their enthusiasm for what turned out to be an epically long night.

We walked to a small bar with an even smaller dance floor haphazardly slapped in the middle. Beer after shot after beer after shot, the guys slammed down their booze with the gusto and resilience of a time-worn Irishman. I was pleased to see Santi had far fewer drinks than his cousins and friends. Part of me hoped my tired eyes and rapid-fire yawns triggered a protective instinct that made him feel the need to watch over me with a clearer mind. I now see that as a fantasy--an unrealistic ideal for our sibling bond.

Between shots and beers, Santi and Antonio took turns asking me onto the dance floor and showing me how to dance merengue, cumbia and bachata. I realized that in Colombia, and possibly in Latin American culture in general, people freely dance with each other, whether they're related or strangers or lovers or anything in between. I pictured myself dancing salsa with my brothers back home in Georgia, and I cringed. *Too weird*, I thought.

Santi tapped my arm at two o' clock in the morning. I had dozed off on his shoulder by then, but apparently it was time to head back home. A cab dropped us off at Tía Cristina's, and I stumbled toward the house. I looked back to see the guys standing idly by the gate. "We're going to a place down the street to keep drinking. Come with us!" said José.

"No way. I'm done. Unlock the gate, please," I said, practically sleep-talking. A turn of the key, and I was in. I hit the bed and dipped straight into five hours of hard-earned sleep.

CHAPTER SIX
Celebrating

I greeted the following morning with raccoon eyes and a case of *aguardiente* breath. A whirlwind of clothes, a splash of hot water and a bite of cheese toast later, I was climbing drowsily into the van that would take us four hours northeast of Bogotá to the city of Duitama, which is located in a region called Boyacá. I squeezed into the car alongside María, José, *Nonita*, Patricia, Patricia's grandmother, Sara, and Kurt. Everyone may have found a seat, but that doesn't mean it was comfortable. Off we went, leaving the boisterous and polluted city behind us. I sunk into my seat, weighed down by exhaustion and by a sense of relief to leave Bogotá's chaotic pace for a day or two. For the first time, I was able to see landscapes outside of Bogotá's mountain ranges. We drove through rolling hills with lush greenery, winding mountain roads framed by towering trees, and smaller-than-life towns that seemed to be plucked straight from postcards. Every few miles, we zoomed past soldiers standing nonchalantly along the roadside with automatic weapons draped across their chests. Every sighting sent a shiver of uneasiness down my spine. I was able to nap for 30 minutes until asphalt led to gravel, and an untimely pothole sent me nosediving toward the seat in front of me. I lurched back just in time. And with that, my nap was over.

Nearing the midpoint of our road trip, the driver pulled into a doll-sized restaurant that sat along the road. The small establishment boasted a corrugated tin roof, a dirt floor and four uncertain walls. We poured out of the car, an entourage of stiff limbs and creaking necks stretching this way and that in the hopes of giving our bodies much-needed mobility. Sara's little hand grabbed mine, and off we went to relieve ourselves.

If the restaurant was tiny, its bathroom was adequately to scale. A toilet filled with urine greeted us, sending me into a gagging fit. The overbearing smell stung through my oversensitive nostrils like a thousand daggers. The space was cramped and I hardly had any room to move. The odor was becoming too much for me to handle. I had made up my mind to run out of that shack as fast as I could when I turned around to see Sara sitting on the toilet, completely unfazed by our surroundings. I wrapped my scarf around my agonized nose. *Do it for Sara. Don't throw up. Don't make a scene.* And so, there I stood, waiting for Sara to finish so that I could barrel through my repulsion and be a model big sister. Somehow, I held it together long enough to relieve myself when Sara had finished. As we left the bathroom, I saw the restaurant owner pour a bucket of water into the toilet, which I realized was the only way to flush the waste. Here, the rule really is "If it's mellow let it yellow. If it's brown flush it down." Growing up, that was a motto we threw around jokingly. It became clear very quickly that this is no joke in Latin America.

Bladders relieved, thirst quenched and bellies full, we were soon back on the road to Duitama. An hour into the second half of our stretch, the van began speaking a special language of *clanks* and *bangs*. Finally, a mysterious puff of black smoke motivated the driver to pull over to examine the issue. He pulled out what I can only imagine was his trusty hammer, crawled under the clown car and began slamming away. Kurt looked at me, eyes wide. "Do you think the van of death will make it to Duitama?" he asked laughing nervously. "Who knows," I said.

About 40 minutes later, Kurt got his answer: No. Luckily, the van broke down 10 minutes from the bride's house, our final destination, and soon a taxi (our knight in yellow armor) came to our rescue to get us through the final leg of what had become a six-hour journey.

* * *

We marched out of the cab upon arrival. I felt like a shell of a human, muscles tense from the crammed car rides and mind worn from a night of drinking that overstayed its welcome. After stretching out on the bride-to-be's couch and taking a few deep breaths, it was time to get ready. Before my visit, María had told me to bring an elegant dress for the wedding. My mom and I saw it as a perfect excuse to spend an afternoon shopping. We wound up at a major department store, where we asked a sales associate for help. As it turned out, she was Colombian. This wonderful woman helped us-- clueless as we were--choose a gorgeous and culturally appropriate dress.

The dress was finally ready for its debut. Patricia pulled me into the bathroom before I could slip it on. On the sink sat a hair straightener and an array of beauty products. She sat me down on the toilet, corralling strands of my thick, unruly hair in order to tame them with the ceramic iron. *No pain, no gain,* I repeated to myself. With my hair set straight, she began applying my makeup. When I was finally allowed to look in the mirror, I saw a beautiful woman smiling back at me. My sleek and shiny hair reminded me of my mother's Southern strands. I wished at that moment she could be there to see my makeover.

After everyone was dressed, we called a cab to drive us to the church. We arrived at the steps of the darling church, painted that special Catholic shade of white and covered with picturesque vines. I took my phone out and snapped a photo. A nun hurried over to me and asked that I shut off my phone with the kind of intimidating grace only a nun can pull off. My cheeks flushed as I put the phone away and apologized for my blasphemous mistake. I walked into the church, where Patricia was waiting to give me my wedding-day instructions.

Apparently, I was to follow her and my younger cousin Ivette, Juanes' sister, to the altar during the ceremony. Patricia explained that my role was to bring flowers to the priest at a specified point during the ceremony. One week into meeting my birth family, and I had already achieved wedding party status. My excitement was dampened only by a fear that I would find a way to give the priest flowers in the wrong moment or in a way that inadvertently offended a church full of my new family members. Patricia handed me my written instructions. Step by step, this piece of paper told me exactly what I was to do with the flowers...in Spanish. I was still unsure of where I needed to take those flowers. My only saving grace was the fact that I was in a church, and if there were ever a time when my prayers could be heard, it was then. *Please don't let me ruin this wedding*, I pleaded silently.

Music filled the church as the ceremony started. I sat in the pews with my legs crossed, channeling the good etiquette my mother taught me. Without explanation, Patricia leaned forward and told me to uncross my well-meaning legs. I felt like a living faux pas. I was thankful Patricia took it upon herself to be my handler. I wondered how many other rules or traditions I was unintentionally disrespecting. The ceremony went on with Sara as their precious flower girl. I was beaming as she tossed the flowers down the aisle with such sass and grace. Then, Patricia, Ivette and I were up. Ivette brought the priest bread as a representation of Christ's flesh. Patricia brought grapes, which symbolized the blood of Christ. And then came my shining moment. My prayers were answered as I walked down the aisle and presented the bouquet to the priest without a hint of sacrilege in sight. I'm still unsure what those flowers were meant to embody.

Once the Mr. had kissed his Mrs., it was my job to pull a confetti popper as they exited the church. Now, *that* was a responsibility I understood and welcomed wholeheartedly. Thirty minutes later, we were on our way to the reception. Before arriving, I decided to throw caution to the wind (along with my heels) and relieve my aching feet by changing into my tennis shoes. It wasn't my most fashionable moment, but at least I could still feel beautiful from head to ankles. We got to the event hall where the reception was taking place, and already the family "paparazzi" were snapping away. Juanes and Gabriela made their rounds, taking photos with a seemingly endless line of parents and cousins and siblings and aunts and friends. I walked over to María, who had already found her place at a table. María is what doctors categorize as morbidly obese. She's spent her lifetime struggling with health issues, including a degenerative eye disease that left her with barely any ability to see. I pulled on her hand, asking her to get up for a moment so that she and I could take a photo with the guests of honor. "I'm too tired," she replied dismissively. *Too tired to walk across the room?* This was my first time celebrating a special occasion with my birth family--during my first visit to Colombia, no less. I walked away in a huff to find someone willing to walk 15 feet in order to capture the moment with me.

The dance floor got rowdier as the evening wore on and the bar poured more drinks. Then it was time for the bride's bouquet to have its moment in the spotlight. All the women (and girls) gathered, eyeing each other like lionesses waiting to devour the only gazelle left in the savanna. Gabriela launched her floral arrangement behind her, and off I leapt, making full use of my cross-trainers for maximum speed and agility. Into my arms flew the arrangement, as we all screamed in delight. Finally, my years of playing sports with my brothers and their friends instead of painting my nails and braiding hair came in handy.

Feeling like a proper champion, I made my way back to the table where my birth mom was still sitting. I dropped the bouquet on the table, knocking one of the white rose buds off its stem. Our driver walked over a few moments later, picked up the lone rose bud and handed it to María. *How sweet*, I thought...until María picked up the bud, grabbed her spoon and started in on the flower as if it were dessert. Her vision had failed her again. Thankfully, she realized it was a flower before taking a bite and began laughing at herself. I felt equally disturbed and sympathetic. I didn't understand why she refused to get glasses.

The party kept going well into the night. Exhausted and slightly bored, Kurt and I watched the hands of the clock tick away as every Latin song blurred into the next. By the end of the night, we danced only to the American songs that inspired us enough to get up off our aching feet and bust a few more moves. I was particularly surprised to hear one song - "Cotton Eye Joe" by a band called Rednex. I was shocked to see all the Colombians dancing to it. The song was a part of my youth - roller rinks played it to draw kids away from the arcade and back to the rink's shiny wooden floors. When the wedding DJ played it, I jumped up and joined everyone on the dance floor. Kurt sat out and opted instead to judge me for knowing all the words, blaming it on me being a Southern girl. I didn't care, it reminded me of where I came from and I was proud.

At one o' clock in the morning, María rallied our group and back to Gabriela's family home we went to pick up our things. I imagined we would stay the night, seeing as how late it was. I was wrong. We were about to embark on that crammed, six-hour drive back to Bogotá...for better, for worse, in sickness and in health.

And so, it was time to climb back into the van, which a mechanic had brought back to life during the wedding. Kurt winked at me as we walked to the car--a signal. He remembered what we had discussed at the reception. If we were going to drive back to Bogotá in the middle of the night, then he and I planned on claiming the backseat. We got to the car ready to claim the ample back row, only to find disappointment. María and Sara had beaten us to the back. I glared at my birth mother and her tiny four-year-old daughter settled into the widest spot in the van like cats curling up for a long nap. I looked at Kurt, whose eyebrows and shoulders rose in tandem. He was right. It was out of our hands.

Instead of stretching out in the ample and in-demand back row, I was forced to squeeze into a small seat with José. I shivered and squirmed my way through the long, frigid drive. A couple hours in, I looked back at María and Sara, who were fast asleep and snuggled under the only blanket in the van. Anger weighed my already heavy eyes down and all I could do was snarl. Kurt caught me simmering, slipped a hand in his pocket and pulled out a pill. "Ambien. It'll help you get some sleep," he said. I couldn't take the sleeping pill fast enough. Two hours later, I still hadn't slept a wink and my teeth had started chattering. Another hour passed and, by then, María had woken up from her deep slumber. I breathed a sigh of relief as she removed the blanket from their laps. *Finally, she's giving it to me.* I froze in disbelief as she wrapped the blanket around her head like a turban instead of handing it to another passenger for a chance at warmth. My blood boiled as I witnessed her selfishness play out. At least I stopped shivering during those heated minutes. I stared out the window for the remaining few hours of the drive, replaying all those moments that had left that taste of disgust, of disappointment, of disillusionment lingering in my mouth--how she wouldn't get up to take a picture with me at the wedding and how little she seemed to care about anyone's comfort outside of her own. Where was her maternal instinct to nurture and comfort me? In that moment, I didn't feel like she was my birth mother--or any kind of a mother figure to me, for that matter. It was close to 7 a.m. when the van pulled up to Tía Cristina's house. I wedged myself out of the car without saying a word and went straight to bed.

CHAPTER SEVEN
Understanding

I slept through most of the day that followed that torturous drive. After dinner, Kurt and I sat in my room talking through everything we had learned about our new families, their cultures, their rituals and their religion. These people, this place, they represented our origin stories, and yet we couldn't have felt more foreign. We laughed at how little any of it made sense to us. We vented about our birth families' irksome habits. My built-up frustration from the night before was still fresh, so it was time to let off the steam. I shared with Kurt how hurt and disappointed I felt that my birth mom hadn't offered me her seat or a blanket, even though I was obviously cold and uncomfortable. Kurt aired his own anger, rehashing how rude it was for his birth mother to continue working while we stood awkwardly in her produce store for hours. "And then she tried to make me feel guilty for leaving! After not giving me the time of day while we were actually there!" he threw his hands up as his voice rose. It felt good to release our frustrations, especially since we each tried to help one another see our respective situations from our birth families' perspectives. And in a small way, it felt cathartic to express myself freely in my own language again.

All of this talk of birth families and different cultures reminded me of the calm, comfortable life waiting for me back home in the U.S. I made my way upstairs and began readying myself for bed. A wave of homesickness hit me as I squeezed my American-brand toothpaste onto my brush. I imagined myself landing at the Atlanta airport and rushing to find my parents waiting for me at baggage claim. I imagined myself hugging them and my mom saying, "We can't wait to hear about your trip!" And my dad chiming in, "Are you hungry?" I missed them. I missed my culture and my way of life. I missed warm showers and flushing toilet paper. I missed sleeping in and smaller meals. I missed my independence. I missed feeling safe. Most of all, I missed speaking English and understanding what people around me are saying!

I had always been proud of being Colombian. In fact, throughout my life I had been prouder of my Colombian heritage than my American upbringing. Being around my birth family helped me understand who I truly am. I am American. I am Colombian. And I am proud to be both.

The next day was Kurt's last in Bogotá, which meant I was about to lose my only American friend and, even more nerve-wracking, my translator. Even though my flight home was still a few days away, I dragged Kurt into the living room to help me discuss the details of my departure with María.

Kurt and I sat down on the couch next to my birth mom, as he explained that I wanted to walk through the logistics for my flight to Atlanta. She seemed surprised when he said this. Her face fell a bit as I told her, through Kurt's translation, what time my flight took off and by what time I needed to be at the airport that day. Admittedly, the conversation was inspired partially by the prior night's quick spell of homesickness, but mostly I felt compelled to take advantage of the little time I had left with a translator of some kind...and, well, an understanding of my birth family's aversion to timeliness.

But after seeing María's reaction to the conversation, I felt bad for bringing it up so many days prior to my actual departure. Kurt then asked if there was anything else I needed to tell her while he was still there to translate. I debated asking about my birth father for a fleeting second. *Not yet*, I decided. It was important to keep the focus of my visit on connecting with my birth mother and this new family that came with her. After all, the reason I set out on the search for my birth mother was so that I could one day thank her for giving me up for adoption. I wanted to let her know how happy and healthy I was. I needed her to know that she did the right thing. That the hardest decision of her life was also the best decision she'd made. I wanted to give her peace of mind and make sure she knew that she did the most loving thing that she could have done for me. And that I loved her for doing it.

"No, that's it," I told Kurt. I knew the right time to talk about my birth father would come, and that wasn't it.

Maybe one reason I never felt the need to learn about my birth father was because there was still so much to learn about the rest of my birth family. One morning, my *Nonita* came downstairs as several of us were eating breakfast. She walked over and rested her hand gently on my shoulder. Time had etched a map of veins, freckles and sunspots onto her small, hardworking hands. She asked Kurt to translate as she proceeded to tell us about her life as a single mother in Contratación, a minuscule town in the Santander region of Colombia. Her eyes shifted downward as she recounted how trying it was to raise seven children whose father (my *Nonito*) not only abandoned them but also who at one point denied the children were his. At this point, María chimed in to tell us that when she was 10 years old her father would sit her down and tell her she wasn't his daughter.

Nonita explained that she would wake up early every day to walk her seven kids to school before spending the day doing physical labor on a farm. At the time, her oldest child was 14 years old and the youngest was just a few months old. "I had to fight to get María into school because of her poor eyesight," she told me. My birth mom was apparently born with optic nerve damage that had caused severe vision problems that had only worsened since birth. According to *Nonita*, María had always scored high on intelligence tests but her school wasn't set up to support a student with limited vision, and so she always struggled through her studies. My birth mom moved to Bogotá when she was 16 years old and began visiting an optometrist every day to learn ways to cope with her vision. It was during María's time in Bogotá that I was born. She was estranged from the family during that time, which is how I remained a secret for nearly two decades.

The focus of the conversation shifted at this point, and *Nonita* looked at me. Her hand caressed my cheek. "I'm so happy you're a part of our family," she said with a sweetness only a grandmother could convey. "But I can't imagine what kind of life you would have had if María had kept you," she continued. She told me how hard things could have been if my birth mom had decided to care for me as a single mother with terrible eyesight, no money, and no support. My birth mom was able to raise Santiago and Sara because, by then, she had a loving and devoted husband and had reconnected with the rest of the family, who helped her tremendously. "I'm very glad you were given the chance to have a good life with your American family," *Nonita* said through a smile. I looked into the kind eyes of this 70-year-old woman whose blood courses through my own veins. The thought of being surrounded by people who shared my gene pool continued to amaze me. I surveyed *Nonita*'s gray hair, pulled back into a neat bun, and sparsely wrinkled face. *Will I look this good when I'm 70?*

* * *

The time finally came for us to say goodbye to Kurt, who was continuing his tour through Colombia. My hug with Kurt lingered as waves of gratitude and sadness crashed against me. I hadn't realized how alone I felt until he arrived-- like a strange creature that accidentally washed ashore on a remote island. I had been surrounded by people since I first stepped foot in Bogotá, so I hadn't felt lonely, per se. It was sharing Kurt's company, sharing his culture, his language, his sense of humor, that lit a spark in me--a small flame that I hadn't noticed go out. I squeezed Kurt and he grimaced, as he does whenever I show him extra affection, and watched with a tinge of loss as he carried on with his own Colombian adventure.

And since life in a capital city of 10 million people waits for no one, my adventure continued to unfold the second Kurt left. My uncle Pepe arrived moments later, and hurried Felipe and me out the door for a day of errands. First, we dropped by Felipe's school to enroll him for the upcoming year. Then, my uncle told me we had to stop by my birth mom's house. A shiver of excitement ran down my spine. I had yet to see María's house since arriving in Bogotá. A part of me felt like I didn't fully know her until I saw where she lived. I wondered if she felt hesitant to invite me into her home because she was ashamed of its size or appearance--both of which are meaningless to me.

We arrived at the house, which was the same size and a similar layout as my Tía Cristina's. My uncle knocked on the door, and soon I could hear the muffled thuds of two small feet running for the door. Sara's coquettish smile greeted us from behind the door as she zestfully shouted *"¡Entren!"* ("come in!") with her signature sass. The house's interior reminded me a lot of Tía Cristina's house, except that Sara escorted us straight up the stairs to the second level. Instead of renting the entire house, my birth mom rents only the second floor. The house is shared by three families, one on each floor. What caught my attention most was the lack of separation between each family's living space. The house was not set up like an American duplex, but rather was simply a three-story home where three families lived. And so, the family on the third floor had to walk through my birth mom's living space in order to come and go from their space. And the family that lived on the ground floor had to feel comfortable with the other two families walking through their space every time they left and entered the house. Each family must trust each other enough to feel comfortable walking through each other's homes every day.

María greeted us at the top of the stairs and showed us around her space. To my surprise, *Nonito* came out from one of the rooms to greet us. "It's so good to see you," he exclaimed as he hugged me. I was taken aback to learn that not only does *Nonito* live with my birth mom, he also has his own room. By then knowing how *Nonito* used to deny that he had children made me see María through different eyes. I admired her ability to forgive.

Sara held my hand as María walked me to her room, where she and Vincente sleep in a double bed. "That's where I sleep!" said Sara pointing to a crib beside the bed. I felt a strange pang at the thought of my sister still sleeping in a crib at the age of four. And yet, there she was, happy as can be and proudly showing off her home. I began to see how a lifetime of privilege had tainted my perspective. As we sat on the bed in María's room, *Nonito* walked into the room with a big smile and his fist clenched around something. He stood in front of me and unclenched his fist to show three coins and a small statue of a woman. He began signaling for me to take them and tried to explain their significance through wild hand gestures. I always had to stop myself from laughing through his fits of charades when he tried communicating with me. All I could make out was that these trinkets were gifts, and the statue was likely of a Catholic saint or some other religious icon. The gift warmed my heart, especially since he was at that point the only male I'd ever met who shared my direct bloodline. There was something about the way he approached me, the way he smiled when he was around me, that made me wonder if *Nonito* still felt guilt or shame for abandoning *Nonita* and his seven children when they were young. It made me wonder if he blamed himself for my birth mother having to put me up for adoption. Something inside of me felt as if those gifts were a form of repentance. A way of apologizing for his past mistakes.

My birth mom then asked if I liked the house and I told her I did. "I wish my home was in a better condition for you," she said. I could feel her shame. I hugged her and said it was lovely the way it was, but I knew she didn't believe me. As I held her close, I leaned into her ear and whispered *"Gracias por todo"* ("Thank you for everything"). Those few words carried a world of meaning.

"Thank you for giving me life."

"Thank you for putting me up for adoption."

"Thank you for giving me the chance to live a full and privileged life."

Unfortunately, all I could muster with my limited Spanish fluency was *"Gracias por todo."* I left it at that and hoped she received the subtext. And apparently, she did. She began to cry after I thanked her, and squeezed me even tighter, which made me cry too. It was the most meaningful and authentic moment I had yet to share with her. In that moment, I remembered my mom in the U.S. I remembered her hugs-- how sweet and wonderful and plentiful they are. How lucky I was to be raised by a woman whose capacity to love has no limits. As I shared that special moment with María, I thought about how this woman sitting next to me, my birth mother, is the reason I was able to meet the woman who raised me, my mother. I continued to cry as I thought about how much my mother meant to me, and how lost I would feel without her. I wished she were there to share in that moment of gratitude and love. I wished she were there to thank María for bringing us together. When I hugged María and thanked her, in my heart, the hug was from my mom, too.

My birth mom then made her way to the kitchen to make lunch. Minutes later, an orchestra of sizzles and chops were accompanied by the fragrant aromas of María's famous cooking. She was cooking lunch orders placed by people who worked around the *centro* where my birth family's shoe store is. María soon came out of the kitchen holding a massive plate of food I assumed was meant for me and Felipe to share. I was wrong. This heaping plate of spaghetti, chicken, fries, and more, was just for me. Of course, it was delicious, but I couldn't fathom eating everything off of that plate, like Colombian culture dictates one must. I told my birth mom about my recent stomach issues, which thankfully helped me get out of finishing my plate. "Why didn't you tell me about your stomach before?" she asked with a glint of concern. I explained that I didn't like discussing anything concerning bodily functions. "Don't be shy about that. We're family. There's nothing to be embarrassed about with family," she responded. "Family." She was right. And it felt good to hear.

Later in the day, after visiting a park and playing on swings and getting ice cream, María, Felipe, Sara and I hailed a cab to make our way back to Tía Cristina's house. The driver cracked a joke when we got in, and everyone began laughing. I couldn't understand what he said, but it felt like he and María were old friends who were sharing an inside joke. I later learned she had never met him. That was something I admired about her: her warmth and friendliness with strangers was what made her a popular presence in her neighborhood. Everyone knew her and everyone loved her. Minutes after the joke was over, she continued chuckling to herself. I smirked. She reminded me of myself in that moment. I have a tendency to keep laughing about something funny long after the moment has passed. *Like mother, like daughter,* I thought.

* * *

The following morning, María arrived in a taxi to pick me up after breakfast. We arrived at the *centro* a few minutes later. María got out of the taxi and walked to the trunk, opened it, and struggled to lift out two large trash bags. A familiar aroma wafted from the bags and carried me toward them. I asked her what was inside. She said *"comida"* (food) with a big smile that made her pillowy cheeks look even more plump. My birth mom had built a small business from her self-taught mastery in the kitchen. The bags, as it turned out, were her way of transporting the nearly three dozen lunch orders placed the day before by business owners, attendants and workers in the vicinity of my birth family's shoe store at the *centro*. We walked around together as she fulfilled orders, first finding the Styrofoam container with the person's name scribbled on the lid, then writing their names, eyes squinted tightly, on a small notepad she carried in her pocket. She would pull the notepad up to her face, hovering only a few inches from her nose, as she jotted each customer's name as an I.O.U. We settled into my birth family's shoe store and as the day continued, her customers would approach every so often to pay for their meal. She would pull out the notepad with each payment and cross the respective customer's name off her list. An unsophisticated system that did the trick. It seemed she could make a decent amount of revenue from each meal served, but I decided not to pry. And anyway, I was still not very good at converting Colombian pesos to dollars. Especially since the conversion rate, at that time, hovered around 2800 Colombian pesos to one American dollar. No matter how much she had made that day, I felt proud of her entrepreneurial mindset.

After helping María pass out lunches, my cousin José *(primo loco)* came to pick me up so we could walk to his dad's restaurant. Apparently, I had yet another uncle who owned a restaurant. It had become increasingly difficult to keep track of all the uncles and cousins and aunts and second cousins and in-laws included in this new family of mine. When we arrived, I greeted my uncle and felt his eyes analyze me as if he was recognizing his sister's features in my own. I smiled and lifted my thumbs as a sign of approval of his small restaurant. He responded with a slanted smirk, as he signaled for us to sit down. José and I settled in moments before a plateful of rice, avocado, flank steak, and an *arepa* found its way in front of us. Nearly every meal comes with a small, white and fluffy *arepa* on the side. I'd come to learn that Colombians use *arepas* to dip into the sauces spilling from their eggs, beans, and meats in the same way Parisians use baguettes. After we finished eating, I snapped pictures of the quaint restaurant and was then summoned to a small grill where I was asked to heat up some *arepas* in preparation for the oncoming afternoon snack rush called *onces*. I moved the uncooked *arepas* onto the stove and wondered if there was a trick to doing this correctly. Primo loco would swoop in every so often to turn an *arepa*, but other than that, I was left to figure out the best method. I must have done an adequate job, because as the *onces* rush began, passersby stopped in to get their afternoon *arepas* and walked away happily enjoying the strings of melted cheese that emerged with each bite. This variety of *arepa* looked like a bread roll filled with ooey-gooey *queso*--very different from the ones my *Nonita* had been serving me, which were much thinner and wider discs of corn *masa* (corn flour) that were served buttered and salted. I must have tried five kinds of *arepas* during this trip, and I was told there are many more, with each Latin American country having their own diverse array of *arepas*.

It was raining by the time we left the restaurant. José and I ran the three blocks back to the shoe store in the rain, passing crowds of people who seemed to nonchalantly carry on with their lives as raindrops gradually covered them. It was a pattern that continued to pique my curiosity--I had noticed it was rare to hear a Colombian complain, especially about trivial matters like rain. When we reached the *centro*, I decided to go upstairs where Santiago, Antonio and Felipe were continuing the daily tedium of wrapping boxes in twine, running shoes up and down three stories, and checking inventory. There's rarely a comfortable place to sit in the tiny eight-square-foot shop, or in the surrounding walkways which are usually packed with people. I figured I would visit with them upstairs and perhaps try to make myself useful.

I turned to the shoe store next to my family's and asked the attendant, Andrés, to help translate between María and I. Thankfully, I'm occasionally able to find an English speaker to help ease the burden of our language barrier. Andrés was a middle-aged man who looked generally weathered by 40-some hardworking years. And yet, a smile always featured prominently on his face. He was a proud funnyman who would meander through neighboring stalls cracking jokes and toying with other owners and attendants. "*Hola, Andrés!* Can you please tell María that I'm going upstairs to sit down, but to please not leave without me?" I asked. He responded with "But of course, *mademoiselle!*" in his heavy accent and even heavier charm. My birth mom responded to Andrés, who let me know that she had asked me to accompany her on an errand before going upstairs. We set off through the bustling streets until, five minutes later, we arrived at a building and got in line for what was clearly its most popular attraction: the elevator.

Ten minutes passed before it was our turn for the big ride. The six people before us piled in, leaving what I thought was just enough room for my birth mom and me. As I took a step forward, the Director of Elevation, as I imagined her title to be, took a sweeping look at María, scanning her from head to toe. She then held a hand up, fingers outstretched, and peered into the line. She called a thin, towering man a few people behind us and asked him to get into the packed elevator in our place. My cheeks flushed as I realized this woman had assumed María was too big, and possibly too heavy, for the at-capacity elevator to handle safely. I felt humiliated by association, as everyone in the elevator and in line witnessed the scene unfold. I felt for María and hoped she didn't feel hurt or embarrassed.

After we had made it into the next elevator, I began to tell my birth mom about how many beautiful-bodied women I had seen in Colombia, and how much less common it was to see such a prevalence of fit women in the U.S. In a way, I guess I was trying to make her feel better about her own weight situation. I was taken aback when she responded to that observation by lecturing me about how much bread and cheese

I was eating. "*Pan con queso* is no healthy. Make you fat!" she said. I found her concern a bit hypocritical considering her own staggering obesity, but I simply nodded in silence and decided to let it go. She then told me that we were running an errand for Tía Cristina, who wins the award for most health and body conscious in the family. The elevator came to a halt at the third floor, where a door immediately to our right led to a room that resembled a doctor's office with its reception desk behind frosted, sliding-glass windows and a to-the-point attendant who wasted no time in asking what we needed. A quick statement from my birth mom sent the attendant on a hunt through the shelves that dominated this secret pharmaceutical garden, but not before sliding the windows shut, as if to shield us from the goodies that lay beyond reach. The window slid open a moment later as the attendant produced a box decorated with flowers, herbs and the before-and-after images of a woman with a bulging belly (the before photo) who apparently slimmed down after drinking this herbal tea (according to the after photo). María then said this is the tea my Tía Cristina drinks to stay thin. I wondered how I could get my hands on a similar tea when I got back to the U.S.

We made our way back to the building's main attraction, and as we waited for the elevator to arrive, two men approached and stood next to us. I'm not sure what possessed my birth mom to strike up a conversation with these strangers, but she was soon sharing with them my earlier comment about women's bodies in Colombia versus those in the U.S. She told them I was from the U.S. and that I enjoyed my fair share of *pan con queso*. The men mumbled something to each other and looked at me with what I could only interpret as pity. In my mind, these men had just said, "Oh what a shame, it looks like she will be another bread-and-cheese-eating fatso then!" All of this talk about weight and body shape was clearly getting to my head. I had always been body conscious, but my stay in Colombia was starting to trigger a near-obsessiveness about my appearance. I felt uncomfortable and irritated by María's sudden urge to share our conversation with these random people. She seemed to think my perspectives were amusing, which only bothered me more. I hated the way those men looked at me, with pity dripping from their pores. Who were they to judge me? When we had finally gotten to the ground floor, I asked if the two men were her friends. She said they were, but with her level of friendliness, it was hard to tell.

Every day, María introduced me to more of her friends (she has so many!). And while it gave my ego a boost whenever she showed me off to her *amigos*, having to plaster a polite smile on my face while she and the friend spoke Spanish and stared at me lost its shimmer after the tenth introduction. I noticed one peculiar pattern emerging from these interactions: her friends never seemed to ask why I didn't speak Spanish or why I lived in the U.S. And, from the bits of conversation I could understand, María never explained that we had been reunited after she had given me up for adoption. This subject was likely a taboo one, but I still found it strange that no one asked where on earth this "new" daughter" came from.

We made our way back to the *centro*, where María settled into her post at the shoe store. She had to finish collecting money from her lunch customers. I was happy to part ways with her by that point, opting for my original plan to spend time with my cousins upstairs.

I spent the time helping my cousin's friend with his work for another store in the *centro*. He was using white paint to cover up marks on the shoes left by the twine they used to bundle shoes for easy transport and storage. Now that these knockoffs had found a willing home, he had to get rid of the stains. I chuckled as he handed me a small foam brush and a can of paint to assist in the cover-up.

Their hard work raised a small red flag in the recesses of my mind. It felt as if I had entered a parallel universe the moment I stepped foot in Bogotá. But back home, reality awaited--more specifically, a jobless reality. I had been watching my teenage cousins and brother work relentlessly every day since arriving in Colombia. All I did was watch them. It reminded me of my privilege. I didn't have a job waiting for me in Atlanta, because I had to dedicate myself to schoolwork. I thought about how much these young men in my family had to sacrifice in order to help their families survive. Instead, I had been able to sign up for 19 hours of classes in the upcoming spring semester, knowing I had my parents' financial and moral support to do so. I imagined what it would be like not have that support system. What if I had had to get a job to survive? It would likely have meant risking my scholarship, my membership in the Honor Society and my high grade point average. It was a sobering realization.

Twenty minutes later, I left the third-floor shoe crew to meet María downstairs, where she had been waiting on me to leave. Through heavy rain and even heavier traffic, we made our way back to Tía Cristina's house (with the herbal goods in tow, of course). Soon after arriving, I crashed for a two-hour nap, waking up to the smell of *empanadas* summoning me to the kitchen. Earlier in the day, I had mentioned to María how much I was craving a beef *empanada* ever since I got one with Kurt a few days prior. Lo and behold, four beef *empanadas* awaited me in the kitchen. I devoured them, even as my aunts told me not to. *"Te vas a engordar!"* ("You're going to gain weight!"), they exclaimed. I replied, "But I'm in Colombia!" as they all laughed. Even Tía Cristina gave me a high five for standing my ground. I was already planning to normalize my eating habits as soon as I got back to the U.S., especially after seeing how many health issues my birth mom suffers through due to obesity. For the first time in my life, I was coming to understand my genetic predispositions. I took María's weight as a warning: I needed to be more careful about my health.

A few minutes later, Santiago was looking through the pictures on my phone. When he found a picture I had taken of María, he pointed to it and asked me "Who is that?" "María," I responded quizzically. He pressed on, "Yes, but who is she?" I stared at him with bemusement. *What is he getting at?*, I wondered. Then, Sara shouted, *"¡Mami!"* and he placed his index finger over his mouth. "Shhh, I asked Mari," he told his little sister. I paused, then said, *"Madre?"* ("Mother?") He laughed and nodded his head, as if I had just won a jackpot prize. I felt strangely off kilter after that random exchange. I didn't know if he wanted me to call her my mom or not. There had been moments between us before that had left me wondering if he resented me for entering their lives abruptly. I had wondered if perhaps he didn't like the idea of sharing his mother with me. This moment only confused me more.

A few minutes later, Vincente, María, Sara and Santiago called a taxi to head back to their home. I walked outside with them to wait for the cab. As we waited, I said *"¡Mira!"* ("look!") as I flexed my legs and invited them to hit my calf muscles to see how strong they were (thanks to many years of dancing ballet as a child and teen.) I was finding the language barrier more frustrating the more time I spent with my birth family. I didn't have the Spanish vocabulary to strike up random conversations or be able to tell them about my hobbies, likes, dislikes, skills, goals, experiences, and dreams. This display of leg strength was my desperate way striking up a conversation to fill the silence and also my way of sharing something about myself with them--no matter how trivial.

CHAPTER EIGHT
Leaving

Four more days. The thought greeted me as I struggled to crack my eyes open after a restful night of sleep. The subtle yearning that had been building in my gut for a couple of days was ready to make itself known as it burst through my subconscious to start the day. I laid there for an hour, anchored to my bed by a quick bout of homesickness until I decided my time, and anxiousness, could be better used to pack one of my suitcases. An hour later, the suitcase was packed and all of my outfits for the rest of the trip were folded into neat piles beside it. Those small acts of anticipation made me feel better--as if doing them somehow got me closer to going back home.

That night, I went to the salon with María and Sara to get our nails done. The small salon was decorated with large posters of models rocking sleek hairstyles with sharply cut bangs and crimson-red streaks. The salon's interior design (and the hairstyles on those posters) harked back to the bubblegum-pop style of the late 90s, so naturally, I felt at home. We were given neighboring seats, at which point Sara planted herself in the middle of my birth mom and me. When it was my turn, I was directed to sit in front of the woman who was going to do my nails. Soon after, Sara sat down at the manicure station next to mine. After sitting there for a while, one of the stylists in the salon passed by me as the manicurist carefully applied a second coat of the deep-red polish to my nails. She ran her fingers through my hair and asked if I wanted to get it done. Without a second thought, I responded *"Si!"* with an immediacy that hinted at my desperation. I hadn't washed my hair since before the wedding, which had been over a week prior. See, the water at Tía Cristina's house only came in two temperature settings: ice-cold and colder than ice. I hadn't dared fully submerge myself in the shower since I had arrived in Bogotá, resorting instead to "splash baths" using the buckets of boiled water given to me each morning. Thus, my hair was a greasy mess of curls that, by then, was screaming for help. I leaned forward, making eye contact with María across Sara's seat, and told my birth mom that I planned to get my hair washed and blow-dried once my manicure was done. "I want my hair done too!" cried Sara in Spanish. María smiled and said "OK," as Sara wiggled her way out of her manicure station and into the hair washing chair.

The warm water coursed across my scalp and down the sides of my forehead. I shut my eyes as the stylist massaged the shampoo into my hair, working it into a sudsy helmet before rinsing and repeating. *Bliss.* When she was done conditioning my hair, she ran her index finger along my eyebrow and asked if I wanted to get them waxed. *Twist my arm,* I thought. I said yes to this master of upselling, as a quick visit to the salon turned into an afternoon at the spa.

I felt like a new woman with my nails painted, hair washed, and brows tamed. I ambled up to the register once we were all set to leave and listened as the "ding!" of the weathered cashier seemed to repeat endlessly. I cringed when the woman behind the register delivered the total cost for all our services. My birth mom had planned to treat us to manicures, and because of me, her bill now included two wash-and-dry hair services and an eyebrow wax. I reached into my wallet and handed María all the money I was carrying to help pay for the spa day. She declined at first, saying it was her gift to me, but I firmly insisted. She finally grabbed the money, and I could feel a wave of relief wash over her.

I had noticed a small voice in my head during the exchange. It seemed to creep up from the deepest recesses of my mind, a part of my subconscious buried under 20 years of ingrained belief systems. That voice spoke up when María took the money. It said, *"She hasn't had to pay for anything for you throughout your entire life. God forbid she pay for one visit to the salon. She owes you this."* But I knew in that moment that the voice wasn't me--it was my trauma, my fear of abandonment. My heart, the real me, knew the truth. And the truth was that María barely made enough money to sustain her family. Just the day before, she had confided that she couldn't afford the Christmas gift Sara wanted. The truth was that my birth family lived in poverty, and she owed me nothing but what she had already given me: the chance to have a privileged life full of love. And so, I was happy to help pay for our afternoon of pampering.

* * *

With the trip coming to a close, I began to ruminate on the many blossoming relationships and new experiences the visit had given me. Of all these new bonds, my new role as a big sister impacted me the most. It was a role I had never known before I met Sara. I grew up with two brothers whose constant masculinity had instilled in me a lifelong dream of having a sister. My heart melted from the moment I saw Sara's picture on Santiago's Facebook profile, an omen for the unconditional love that was yet to develop. The visit to Bogotá brought me to reality's doorstep. The sisterly relationship I had romanticized became a nuanced, real-world connection. That little bundle of energy and sass charmed me, annoyed me, frustrated me, entertained me, angered me and softened me, all during my short stay in Bogotá. I don't think anyone had ever told me they loved me as much as Sara did. I also never thought I'd grow tired of hearing someone tell me they loved me until Sara said it for the five-hundredth time.

Still, I felt so grateful for her. How many people can say their dream of having a little sister came true overnight when they were 21 years old? Sara is one of the many gifts that came from my adoption. Our bond seemed to grow stronger with each day that I was in Bogotá. At one point, it seemed like I was the only one she would listen to. She wouldn't put her coat on for anyone else. She would only sit on *my* lap. She would only hold *my* hand. She wanted to be with me and do everything *I* was doing at *all* times. She amused and exhausted me. That's the reality of any relationship--they're complex and multifaceted and unpredictable. And I wouldn't have it any other way.

In the short time I had known her, I had already started forming a laundry list of hopes and fears for her. *I hope she does well in school. I fear for her safety. I hope she finds success in life. I fear someone will disappoint her. I hope she learns English. I fear she'll never understand me. I hope she visits me in the U.S. I fear she'll one day forget about me.*

* * *

The next morning, my eyelids flew open to an orchestra of barking dogs and car alarms accompanied by megaphone-clad vendors and featuring Tía Marcela's hum solo as she mopped outside my room. She played her own symphony of banging handles and clanging buckets.

I huffed as I got out of bed. *One more day until I get my privacy back.* I stepped into the hallway, and by the time I realized the floor was still wet, my knee had hit the ground. *Ouch!* Sara had just walked out around the corner when she saw me slip. Her first instinct was to laugh at me, but when she saw me rubbing my knee, face contorted with pain, she *actually* put the smartphone down, asked me where it hurt and then rubbed my knee with her little hand. She asked if it felt better. *"Si, gracias,"* I replied, and she gave me a kiss. I thought it was a really sweet gesture on her part.

Tía Marcela reached into the freezer to grab ice for my knee when she said...well, I didn't quite understand what she told me specifically, but it may have translated into something about my birth mom offering to buy me a pair of shoes later that day. Perplexed, I nodded in agreement as if I understood all of her Spanish (something I find myself doing often). The taxi pulled up 30 minutes later to take me to the *centro*. At the shoe store, I watched the morning turn into the afternoon. Everyone seemed to have something to do but me. Santiago and Antonio were off on an errand and weren't there for me to watch them work, so I let Tía Cristina know that I was going to my uncle's restaurant to visit my cousin Patricia. Patricia had made a real effort to build a relationship with me since I had arrived, but her work schedule kept getting in the way. Patricia had even changed her Facebook profile picture to a photo of her and me. Another picture of us together featured prominently on her phone's home screen. It was flattering to see how much she cared for me. I cared for her, too.

I walked the short route to the restaurant alone, which was one of the crowning achievements of my trip. Not needing an escort made me feel like a true Colombian. I seemed to blend into the masses like a local. After all, I am Colombian by blood so, as long as I kept my very American mouth shut, nobody would know the difference. In fact, while growing up in the United States, many of my fellow Americans would assume that I spoke Spanish because of how I look. Latinos living in the United States often speak to me in Spanish and I feel embarrassed when I don't know how to reply. I have a memory of being in Middle school and a Colombian girl in my class told me I wasn't a "real" Colombian since I didn't speak the language. It hurt. So, walking down the street to my uncle's restaurant all by myself in the capital of Colombia made me feel a sense of belonging that I wasn't accustomed to back home, and it felt like a big deal. I got to the restaurant and made my rounds visiting my uncle and cousins. It felt strange, not knowing if I would see them again before I left.

Santiago dropped by as I sat down to a plate of food. He flashed me a coy smile. *"Que?"* ("What?") I asked. *"Mira!"* ("Look!") he said as he opened his mouth to reveal a shining object. He had gotten a tongue ring. A small, oddly placed tongue ring. Apparently, he didn't want to be like every other rebellious teenager who had gotten a tongue ring to feel independent. And so, he had gotten it done on the right side of the tip of his tongue. I rolled my eyes. He told me not to say a word to anyone about his piercing. At least he trusted me enough to let me in on his little secrets.

* * *

Once I had spent some time at the restaurant, I was back on my way to the shoe store, where María was apparently going to take me around to find a pair of shoes (according to what I think Tía Marcela said earlier when she was icing my knee in the kitchen). I got to my birth family's shop, and Antonio pointed upstairs. "María is waiting for you on the fourth floor," he said. This is usually where Santiago and Antonio work on "cleaning" the shoes and managing the shop's inventory. The elevator was broken, so I had to walk up the four flights of stairs. Breathing heavily, I thought about how my birth mom had to make this trek to look for me, which couldn't have been easy at her size. *This is the kind of strenuous exercise she needs more of,* I thought. She was sitting in a small area enclosed by piles of shoes on the fourth floor when I finally arrived, with a slight dew on my forehead from the climb. She got up and said something as she started laughing, but I only understood the word *"gato"* ("cat"). I must have looked incredibly confused, because as Antonio surfaced from the staircase, he asked my birth mom what was going on. *"Gato"* came up again as she apparently explained what she had said. He chuckled and told me she said that she and I had been playing a game of cat and mouse as we tried to find each other. This had become commonplace: a statement made in Spanish followed by my utter confusion followed by the search for a translation, and all to learn that what had been said was a passing, and often useless, comment. It was one of the more frustrating patterns of my visit.

I then mentioned to my birth mom that Tía Marcela had said something about shoe shopping. Again, this may not have been an actual plan since I couldn't fully understand what my aunt had said, but the fact that I brought it up sent María on a mission to find me shoes, thinking that I had to have a pair right then and there.

We walked down the four-story staircase, and within 20 minutes, I had found my new footwear. A crimson-red platform propped up the leopard-print stiletto to create a striking replica of the sky-high pumps that usually tread the red carpets. I had never owned shoes that sexy. *Hey, I'm in Colombia,* I figured. *Go big or go home.* And as it turned out, I planned to do both. María walked up to the store owner and handed him three bills of what looked like the largest denomination I recognized. My cheeks reddened as I realized that I hadn't thought to ask their price. I felt a pit of guilt in my stomach that was only reassured by how insistent she had been about buying them for me. Apparently, it was her plan after all. I made sure she knew how grateful I was for the gift. She smiled and squeezed my hand in response. I could tell she enjoyed being able to treat me to the things I liked, and that meant the world to me.

And the pampering continued when I mentioned being a bit hungry. María told me to follow her as she immediately set off, walking outside of the *centro* and down the street to a *tienda* that pulled us in with the smell of freshly used fryers. She ordered two *empanadas* for me, which I promptly doused in hot sauce and scarfed down. Unfortunately, the hot sauce my taste buds craved also triggered a vengeful attack in the form of acid reflux. Acid reflux is nothing new to me, and it's my body's way of telling me to stop overeating. I had noticed myself consuming food compulsively for a few days in tandem with heightened levels of stress. I could feel a ball of anxiety forming in my stomach as the countdown to my departure drew nearer, and I had turned to food to try to numb the tightness in my gut that grew only more uncomfortable.

Acid reflux aside, María and I continued our little adventure as we stopped into a store owned by her friend so that she could introduce me. Her friend ran toward us, lunging forward to squeeze me between her well-cushioned arms. She spouted a few things in Spanish, her pitch and tone translated joy, and the tears she had gathered by the time she pulled away from me told me she was gushing about my being back in María's life. My birth mom shed a few tears as I kept picking up on her friend saying things like *"Dios"* ("God") and *"felicidad"* ("happiness") and *"bendición"* ("blessing"). She said all of this while staring at me, eyes wide and hands cupped over her mouth in awe. It was hard not to react to his kind of emotional display. I held back my one or two rogue tears, opting instead for a wide smile. I didn't want to break down in front of total strangers. I had a feeling that I wouldn't have been able to turn off the tears had I allowed them to flow in that moment. I ignored the lump in my throat and gave María a tissue to wipe her tears.

We left the store once everyone's tears had been shed and noses had been wiped. As María and I walked, she grabbed my hand and looked at me with the kind smile of a doting mother. And yet, all I could think about was the sweaty palm that now encased my right hand. I cringed internally, which was then followed by feelings of guilt for this involuntary repulsion that consumed me nearly every time she held my hand. This wasn't a reaction to my birth mom, per se. This was a reaction to germs. I'll admit I'm a bit of a germaphobe. The feeling of a moist hand makes the hairs on the back of my neck stand at attention. During my time in Bogotá, I noticed how even my own hands were noticeably dirtier throughout the day. I wasn't used to seeing grime under my nails until that trip. I chalked it up to the air pollution but couldn't figure out exactly what the deal was with the extra dirt on my hands. I could see María staring at me curiously each time I slathered hand sanitizer from the tips of my fingers to well below my wrists. I used hand sanitizer before and after eating, and several times throughout the day. We continued walking to the shoe store, and perhaps to make up for my clean-freak faux pas, I grabbed her hand and told her that I loved her.

She smiled. "I love you, too. Don't forget about me, Mari." Her grip on my hand tightened. "Promise me you'll come back." Her eyes betrayed her desperation.

"*En Junio*" ("In June"), I responded, almost involuntarily. In an email they had sent me the day before, my parents mentioned returning to Colombia with me in June. It was far from a concrete plan, and frankly, in that moment June seemed too soon for a return visit.

This wasn't the first time questions about my next visit had come up. In fact, my birth family asked me about it every day. "Soon," I'd say. And then, without fail, they would ask if I ever planned on bringing my parents with me. I had grown accustomed to explaining that I very much wanted to return with my mom and dad one day. I wanted them to meet my birth family. I wanted them to get to know the woman that birthed their daughter, and the people whose genes I shared. I wanted them to get to know Sara and see how much she and Santiago look like me. But I was nervous that the cultural differences would create tension and the language barrier would cause frustration. I don't think my birth family understands the vast difference in cultures like I do. Even in college, I learned about different cultures and their customs. I had learned that Latin American cultures tend to prioritize family and friendship above all else. Meanwhile, American culture emphasizes the importance of career success, schooling and adhering to schedules. With the cultures being so different, I feared that my birth family would interpret my vague responses as disinterest rather than what it truly was: uncertainty about my schedule and how I would afford a second trip.

Of course, I wanted my birth family to meet the people who raised me. I would often fantasize about my two families meeting, chuckling at how much more sense I would make to my birth family once they saw my American upbringing in action. What they may have interpreted as my quirks may end up being only cultural. I had wondered how my birth family would feel to see me with my parents. I dreamed of one day visiting FANA, my adoption home, with my parents. I had always fantasized about being the one to present a baby to its new adoptive family. It's a time-honored FANA ritual to allow older adoptees the honor of doing this when they return to the home. On many occasions, I had imagined what a special and emotional experience this could be for anyone lucky enough to live it.

Finally, when my birth mom asked me when I was returning, I had a more definite answer, even if it was premature. I didn't want to give her false hope by saying I could return in June, but I also didn't want to keep giving the same vague answers so I was glad to finally have a better response than "no sé" ("I don't know").

The conversation about my return would inevitably turn into a discussion about my birth family visiting me in the United States. María and my Tías kept asking if they could stay with me and my family during their hypothetical trips to Atlanta. *"Claro que si,"* ("Of course") I responded each time with false confidence. The truth was, I didn't know how my parents would feel about hosting my birth family in their home. If I know anything about Lisa and Pete Andersen, it's that they are open, warm and loving people who would do anything to make the people in my life happy--but only after meeting them in person.

I knew my parents and I would visit Colombia together soon enough. But for now, I couldn't wait to go home.

* * *

The day had finally come. It was time to head back to the U.S. after meeting my birth family for the first time during a two-week adventure in Colombia. My alarm rang at 5:30 that morning. I don't think I have ever showered, eaten breakfast, and gotten myself ready as fast as the morning of my departure. I had grown more restless each day leading up to my last. The night before leaving, I was consumed by the image of myself stepping off the plane and onto American soil, where my parents were waiting to hug me. I wanted to be with my people again. I wanted to fit it again.

I was tired of feeling like a fish out of water.

Tired of everyone speaking Spanish.

Tired of breathing in exhaust fumes.

Tired of having to watch my back.

Tired of not being allowed to put my hands out the car window.

Tired of having to be quiet in public so no one would hear my American accent.

Tired of forcing myself to eat whether or not I was hungry.

Tired of never knowing where I was going.

All I wanted was to be back in a familiar environment. All I wanted was to feel understood.

As I had predicted, the goal of getting me to the airport by 7 a.m. turned out to be a far-fetched dream. It didn't matter though because I got to the airport and I wasn't going to miss my flight. My birth mom clung to me as we walked with Santiago, Antonio, Sara and Tío Pepe through the airport. María held onto my hand tightly and would hook her arm into mine every so often. *Just let her*, I told myself. We only had a few minutes together, of course she wanted to be close to me. And yet, once again, my immediate reaction was to pull away from her. To keep my distance. In that moment, I wished I could have allowed myself to embrace her love for me instead of running away from it. I wished I knew how to silence the subconscious voice that kept telling me to pull away from her. I wished I could make sense of it.

We had some time to spare after I had checked my luggage and received my boarding pass. Gorgeous little shopping stalls line Bogotá's El Dorado Airport, which gave me the perfect excuse to squeeze in a last little shopping spree. I headed into a small shop lined with hand-stitched leather bags and jewelry made with Colombian gold. There were magnets decorated with Colombia's most famous symbols: *chiva* buses and *campesinos* (farmers) and *haciendas* (plantations). So many things caught my eye that reminded me of this incredible trip. I picked out a ring made out of ivory or something similar. As I brought my trinket to the register, Tío Pepe swooped in and paid for the ring. This final gesture made my heart swell. My birth family was nothing if not generous. Each time I had mentioned wanting something--be it shoes or jeans or *empanadas* or this ring--they had gone to great lengths to get it for me. This meant even more since, for two weeks, I had witnessed how hard they all worked just to put food on the table.

My birth mom had begun pressing me to move things along as my ring was being wrapped in tissue paper at the gift shop. I wondered if she wanted to get the goodbyes over with, like ripping off an old bandage that had formed a close bond to the skin.

Anyhow, I had never been good at goodbyes, so I was thankful that she also seemed to want to be done with it. We stood face to face as the inevitability swept over us. She moved toward me, arms wide and face contorting as a stream of tears made their entrance. We both cried together, our arms intertwined. She whispered in my ear, *"Te quiero mucho."* (I love you so much). *"Yo también"*, I said through shallow breaths.

When Sara approached, my eyes grew heavier. She ran into my arms, in only the way a child does, and held me tight. It was hard saying goodbye to Sara, even though the night before she had said she loved my cell phone more than she loved me. Someone must have had the "Phones are not more important than people" talk with her, because she seemed more willing to love me despite my inability to play YouTube videos for her at the airport. Sarcasm aside, I wondered if Sara truly understood what was going on in that moment. Of course, she knew I was leaving in a basic sense. But had she understood what my visit meant? I wondered if she would feel abandoned by me once I left. I wondered if she would even notice. My insecurities were getting the best of me again.

Santiago and I both cried when we said goodbye. My throat gets tight just thinking about it. I had only recently found out that I had a brother four years younger than me. And literally overnight, there I appeared in his life--a walking embodiment of his mother's lifelong lie. I entered his home, played with his little sister, held his mother's hand. Of all these new family members, it was the relationship with my half-brother that had been the hardest to navigate. And yet, I felt bonded to him in ways that I couldn't explain. It felt like, through all the turmoil of this uncharted territory, there was a strong current of love that carried us forward. I looked into his eyes as we said goodbye. So much of our closeness remained unspoken but nonetheless understood.

My heart ached as I looked at each of my new family members one last time. We had all shed our tears as the bandage was ripped painfully off. As I turned away to walk to my gate, I wiped my eyes and readied myself for the long-anticipated journey back home. Although my heart was heavy, the thought of hugging my parents at the Atlanta airport brought me a pang of joy so intense it brought tears to my eyes again. This time, I cried at the thought of the hellos that awaited me on the other side of my five-hour flight.

I stared out of the window as the plane lifted from the runway. The higher it went, the more my heart hurt. I watched the city of Bogotá drift away from me gradually. I replayed the past two weeks. I thought about the people there. I thought about how much I cared about them, and how they cared about me. As ready as I was to be home, I knew I would miss them terribly.

CHAPTER NINE
Homecoming

My lungs filled with oxygen and my eyes filled with tears as the plane touched down in Atlanta. I did my best to stay calm until I was with my parents and able to unleash these built-up emotions. As I headed toward the area where all of the passengers' loved ones wait, I scanned the crowd with desperate eyes to find my mom and dad. When I finally spotted them they felt like a mile away, so I sped toward them. As the gap between us closed, I burst into tears. My parents opened their arms to embrace me as their eyes also filled with tears. My heart was overflowing with relief, gratitude, and the feeling of home as they wrapped their arms around me. I am so indebted to these two people. It was because of them that I was given the opportunity to live the life I have today. Every watery tear that fell from my face was acknowledgment of my newfound gratitude. How could I ever express to them the revelations my Colombian adventure provided me? I wasn't certain, but I knew I would find a way.

Giddy to be reunited, my parents and I went to lunch so I could narrate to them all the details of my life-changing experience and show them a few of the thousand-or-so of pictures I had taken. The gratitude I initially felt at the airport swelled as I experienced the comfort and ease of eating at a restaurant in the United States. There were things I would never again take for granted. I drank water from a cup. I chose what I wanted to eat. I easily conversed with the server. Until now, I had not realized the full extent of the anxiety I had accumulated on my trip. Each little moment of relief eased a piece of what had been my invisible burden. I was home. I felt unrestrained comfort for the first time in weeks. Little did I know, the sweetness of my arrival would soon see its end.

The same night I returned home, my boyfriend broke up with me. Although I knew it was coming, this added a new layer to my state of emotional whiplash. He had shown a darker side of himself when I was visiting with my birth family. We had entered a constant and toxic state of arguing. My access to the Internet was limited in Colombia, but the times we did spend chatting were filled with accusations that I was selfish. Selfish? This was the most transformative experience of my life. What had he expected? I was eager to share these life-changing moments with him, while it seemed he was more eager to leave me feeling bruised with guilt. I had tried to stay optimistic. *We'll work it out when I'm back home,* I had repeated to myself like a mantra. But I was wrong. My recently unburdened heart sank quickly into a depression.

The combination of returning home, my breakup, and the Christmas holidays left me reeling. I tried to stay focused despite feeling so disoriented. *Remember to call your birth family and wish them a Merry Christmas,* I told myself. I kept reminding myself the importance of this, but my mental state was cloudy and my heart was heavy. I took solace in the sweet excitement my family expressed upon seeing the pictures from my trip. My parents, older brother, his girlfriend and my grandparents sat through exactly 1,167 pictures. They greeted every picture with a smile. Finally, I could share the joy I experienced in Colombia.

I managed to call some members of my birth family on Christmas Eve, but my enthusiasm was minimal. The fuzzy cloud encircling my head made me unsure about how I felt about almost everything. Even opening presents on Christmas morning didn't excite me. The new digital camera I received sat forgotten in its packaging. My attachment to material possessions had evaporated. I was lost in my own fog.

* * *

I reconnected with my friends from high school in an attempt to ground myself. I was processing an array of complex emotions and I needed help sorting through them. My mind felt like a maze. Moments of normalcy and unapologetic conversations brought me glimpses of strength. I wasn't certain how to describe the feelings I was experiencing. I wished I had a superpower that could play the mess in my head like a movie to those around me. I existed in a dual reality. I would feel myself drift away mentally to Colombia, only to be yanked back to the present when my friends called my name. I opened up to a few of my closest friends about the raw, vulnerable moments I experienced on my trip. Their uncertain "hems" and "haws" in response did nothing to soothe me or make me feel understood. It was unfair of me to expect them to relate to my experience, but I so desperately wanted them to. I felt alienated, separated from what was once so much a part of me. Loneliness crept in. I wondered if I would ever feel like I belonged to something again.

* * *

Every sunrise brought me closer to reconciling my feelings from the trip. Fresh perspectives crept into my outlook. The further I got from it, the more I realized how perfectly timed my breakup had been. I abandoned my need for immediate clarity and dutifully accepted the journey I was on. *Carpe diem* (live in the present). That saying made more sense. I felt myself waking up from the haze of the past few months as a new beginning dawned. I was awake. I was aware. I was alive. I was thankful.

After the holidays, I trekked back to my sleepy college town of Valdosta, Georgia, to resume my daily life. I did my best to apply my refreshed outlook to this next chapter. I channeled the forward-looking Colombian mindset. In Colombia, no one seems to worry about the what ifs or maybes. Colombians live vibrantly immersed in the present.

They exude a kind of indisputable trust. *Que sera, sera* (What will be, will be). They relinquish control more easily than most of the Americans I know. They surf on the current of the Universe and accept life as it comes, whether that manifests as a high or low tide. This attitude became my inspiration.

The drive to Valdosta seemed to advance in slow motion. I was anxious to get back. The end of this commute signified the beginning of my adjustment to this new life. *Can't I just arrive already?* My patience had all but disappeared when I pulled into a gas station and saw a woman, doused in dust and weakened by hunger or something far greater. She held a tattered cardboard sign. "Homeless and hungry" was scribbled onto the sign in thick black ink. I tried not to stare as I walked into the gas station, where my anxiety led me on a Supermarket Dash-style spree for chips and a sandwich and a soda and sunflower seeds, and really anything else that could squash my hunger while also taking my mind off the maddening hour left of my trip. The station attendant bagged my loot, and off I went back to my car. As I walked by this woman again, I stared at her sign then at the bag of food I had just bought. I remembered the starving people and animals on the streets of Bogotá. I remembered how desperately I wished I could help them. I grabbed the turkey sandwich out of the plastic bag and handed it to this homeless woman, who was here, in my home, in my country.

I hoped my small act of kindness satisfied her hunger, as it certainly satisfied my desire to understand my first-world privilege. This moment felt designed to remind me of my bountiful life. I felt for the woman who seemed to have so little. And, soon, my anxiety turned into gratitude, which turned the dark cloud over my head into a ray of sunshine. Negativity had been a constant thread woven into my life before Colombia. Growing up, I was picked on by neighborhood boys which led to me bullying myself for having more curves than the skinny white girls around me. Now, I could see the Colombian mountains in the robust geometry of my shape. For the first time in my life I was ready to embrace myself fully, my body, my opinions, and the depths of what makes me who I am.

I hoped to carry some of that positivity into the first class of the semester the next morning. Armed with the only thing that felt right, blind faith, I prayed that this was the beginning of an upward spiral. By trusting the flow of the universe, I knew I was opening myself up to the limitless possibilities that come with every new path. Cramming 19 hours and seven classes into my schedule would certainly be a test of this newfound positivity. I told myself busy would be good for me.

* * *

Only three weeks had passed, and yet it seemed as though epiphanies were raining down on me every day since my return. First, came my understanding of the power of blind faith. Learning to let go and trust the process of life was the only way I came to embrace my new beginning--my life after meeting my birth family, my second family, my new identity. The next epiphany was just how accepting and gracious the Colombian culture is compared to the more judgmental American way of life. I had noticed during my time in South America that Colombians tend to speak to one another as equals. They see the humanity in each other. They acknowledge the suffering and celebration of all people, regardless of what designer bags or shoes they have. Which brings me to my next epiphany--a one-two punch, of sorts. I realized that I was the person with the designer bags and shoes. And, with that, I had to come to terms with the harsh fact that I had spent my entire, privileged life without an ounce of awareness of just how entitled I was. Seeing that kind of tainted reflection in the mirror can be startling and disheartening, but it was necessary. I had to face who I was-- who I had been--in order to become who I was meant to be.

Flaunting labels in a metropolis like Atlanta isn't just commonplace, it's encouraged. The more decked out you are in designers, the better--especially in ritzier neighborhoods like Buckhead. But I found the opposite to be true in places like Bogotá and Valdosta. Wearing my privilege in South

Georgia had a surprisingly alienating effect. When I wore my matching Coach shoes and purse to class during the early part of the semester, I could feel the tension in the room grow as my classmates' eyes lingered on my shoes and then slowly lifted to my purse in unison, as if following the counts of an invisible conductor. I could practically see "snob" trying to fight its way out of their pursed lips. I felt immediately quarantined, an especially unpleasant state for someone as extroverted as I am. Another world where I didn't belong. It looked like new friendships weren't in my near future. *Fine,* I told myself resolutely, *I'll have more time to focus on myself.*

As it turned out, my trip to Colombia prepared me amply for coping with being scrutinized by strangers and other challenges I would confront while adjusting to life in small-town Georgia. Before leaving for Colombia, I remember my mom had warned me about the slower pace I would confront while there--she suspected I would find it difficult to decelerate my naturally up-tempo rhythm. And she was right. Colombians take their sweet time even amongst the hustle and bustle. I was raised with the fast-paced American spirit, so this change had me constantly hunting for patience and practicing restraint through stillness.

In Valdosta, I was waist-deep in a completely different kind of culture shock--the jarring down-tempo of rural American life. My Colombia-bestowed patience was put to the test upon my arrival in South Georgia. *Find your stillness,* I would remind myself. Another epiphany was how I used to just take things at face value. Taking a beat allowed me to assess the reasons behind people's actions. Colombia helped me step back, analyze, and relate--or let it go. I was learning to rely on myself completely and with confidence. I didn't have any friends to lean on in Valdosta. This tiny town was closed off to the world and steeped in old-world Southern culture. Often, living there felt like the ultimate test of my resilience and positivity. That small corner of the world became the garden where I grew a crop of fresh epiphanies. And while I was powerfully cultivating my capacity for self-respect and self-worth, at the end of the day, I still had no one with whom to share my victories.

* * *

I had only spoken to my birth family once since returning home from Colombia. Several weeks into my return home, and just a week into my move to Valdosta, I video-called my birth mom for the first time since my trip. Her face contorted in surprise as she answered the call. She was clearly upset that I hadn't called sooner. Sure, I hadn't spoken to her in three weeks, but the sheer shock in her voice made my face turn sour. How could she question the depths of my love for her and the rest of my birth family? How could she possibly think I had forgotten about them? I had thought about them every hour of every day. I felt insulted. As if the bond we had worked to build while I was there just up and vanished. But it wouldn't help the situation if I brought all of this up to her, so I brushed it off. Long-distance communication can be so easily derailed. She told me that Sara had been talking about me all the time. Apparently, Sara even walked around the house with her mom's phone to her ear pretending I was on the other end. It warmed my lonesome and homesick heart to think about that four-year-old little bundle of personality missing me, her sister.

That had been the last time I spoke with my birth mom for a while, or anyone in my birth family, for that matter. My days had become occupied with training to become an American Sign Language interpreter. Sometimes, it felt as though Colombia had been a dream. The memories of the trip were becoming out of focus. Soon, I was struggling to recall the details. One month had passed since I had last wrapped my arms around the members of my birth family. I found myself wishing I had spent just a few more minutes with them at the airport in Bogotá before rushing off to my gate. Homesickness--if you can call it that--ransacked my heart. Had Bogotá become my home? I missed it, and my people there, beyond words. But I also missed my family and my true home--if you can call it that--in Atlanta. I couldn't pinpoint which home I missed more. I missed the warmth and comfort of my family in Atlanta, but I missed the obvious genetic connection I shared with my birth family. My heart was split between Atlanta and Bogotá, but instead I lived in the one place where my heart was not...Valdosta. I kept myself distracted in an effort to keep the pain of longing at bay. Distraction was the best coping tool I could find. My hunch had been right--keeping busy was keeping me sane.

CHAPTER TEN
Returning

It had been a whole year since I found my birth mother with the help of Carolina and just six months since I first stepped foot on Colombian soil. The days since my trip had turned into weeks. Weeks had bled into months. My life in Valdosta looked about the same as it did when I first moved there, except as time passed, I had something to show for all of the solitude: strong grades. I was excelling in school, which made my struggle to adjust all the more worthwhile. Time I had spent analyzing and processing transformed into positive action and energy. I knew I needed to set myself up for a successful future and that was the time. Throughout those six months, I picked up yoga, began practicing meditation, and embraced the practice of living in the moment. I felt spiritually awakened.

It wasn't long after my return to the U.S. that my parents and I began planning our return to Colombia--this time together. That small-town chapter of my life had transformed me into a better version of myself. Mari 2.0 felt ready to take on the world, starting with a second visit to my country of origin. I would fly out in one week, and my parents would meet me there a week later. It was time to set my two worlds, my two families, and my two contrasting realities on a collision course.

Preparing for my trip was much easier the second time around. It was nice to be free of the panicky anxiety that built steadily as my last trip drew nearer. Emotionally, I felt surprisingly calm this time. *Maybe it's all the yoga I've been doing?* As I prepped my suitcases, I thought back to what I had brought with me last time. During my first visit, I dressed casually to avoid sticking out--but that backfired. I ended up looking disheveled next to the perfectly primped women of Bogotá. I wouldn't make that mistake again. This time, I wanted to bring cuter clothes that made me feel put together. I had learned so much during my first visit. I knew my second adventure would rely on me living in the moment and releasing preconceived expectations. Of course, I still had my list of concerns. I worried that my parents' desire to sightsee might conflict with any plans my birth family may have made. I worried that miscommunications would create tension. I worried about the language barrier--my Spanish was a little better, but not by much, and my parents don't speak a word of it. The lack of control would certainly still prove frustrating. Still, all I could think about was seeing my birth family's smiling faces again. I needed to trust that everything would work out the way it was supposed to.

I planned to do more than just visit family during my second visit. I also planned to dig into the two remaining gaps in my origin story.

First, I wanted to see FANA for myself. I wanted to step foot inside the orphanage where my life forever changed--the place where I was adopted, where I met my mom and dad, where I became an Andersen. I had fantasized for months about sharing that experience with my parents, and how special it would be for us to be there together for the first time since they adopted me at five weeks old. My first trip to Colombia made black and white documents come to life in vibrant, tactile colors. On this second trip, these two additional pieces to my story would bring those colors into sharper focus.

The other gap in my story wasn't as easy to fantasize about as a visit to FANA. It wasn't as clear-cut. It wasn't as celebratory. It was my birth father. I was on the fence about whether I wanted to meet or even search for him. I initially thought I had no interest in finding him, but my curiosity had been getting the better of me. With information ready to surge at the touch of a button, I knew modern technology would lead me down an instant rabbit hole of investigation if I ever learned his name. It would likely be a slippery slope from there. As much as Mari 2.0 was a new and improved version, she also carried a lot of the fundamental characteristics of Mari 1.0--insatiable curiosity among them. Regardless of what I uncovered, I would never respect him like I did my birth mother. I could never forget how he abandoned her while she was pregnant, poor, alone, and just barely an adult. My birth mother never mentioned him, and I didn't blame her for that. The thought of asking her about him put my stomach in a knot. I hoped that, if I did decide to ask, she would understand that it was because I wanted to know about the other half of the story. I worried she would take offense, or worse, that she would think I was unfulfilled by our relationship. I would have to be delicate and tactful. But first, I had to decide if I even wanted to know.

* * *

The flight back to Bogotá went smoothly. I was filled with a happy excitement that kept a smile on my face nearly all of the five hours as I relived moments from my first trip nostalgically. As soon as the plane touched down in Colombia, I ran to the bathroom to throw on my *ruana* in order to reunite with my family in proper Colombian style. I arrived at the customs desk, and this time I proudly flashed my crisp, new Colombian passport, courtesy of the Colombian consulate in Atlanta. I beamed with pride as the officer stamped my passport without a single question or doubt. *This is what it feels like to belong.* I made my way to baggage claim, and there they were. My birth family's gleaming faces crowded the glass wall. There must have been 15 people there to receive me. My heart was beating out of my chest as I scanned each of their familiar faces, giddy with anticipation. I snapped up my luggage, and practically ran to the exit, where they were now waiting for me. Our reunion was a parade of hugs and kisses as I was passed around to each member for a one-on-one welcome.

I jumped in the car with José, *primo loco*. Sara had been curled up in the backseat sleeping tenderly until I opened the car door. Her face surged with joy as her sleepy little eyes peeled open. She lunged toward me, and I held onto her without any plans for letting go. She pulled me into the backseat with her, and interlaced her small, delicate fingers with mine. The sisters were reunited. We held hands the entire ride back to María's house. There, we dropped off Sara, my birth mom and Vincente, and then headed back to Tía Cristina's house, where I would be staying again. I walked through the door of my aunt's house, and in true *Nonita* style, three *empanadas* and a Coca-Cola waited for me on the kitchen table. My heart was full and, now, so was my belly. I felt at home.

During my first visit, I stayed in my cousin Felipe's room while he bunked with his brother. This time, they walked me upstairs to a room on the top floor, where two twin beds were neatly made up. Tía Cristina pulled my luggage next to one bed, and then explained that my parents were going to share the other when they arrived in a few days. A lump gathered in my throat, as I tried to envision my king-sized parents squeezing onto a twin-sized bed. I felt responsible for their comfort. I had convinced them to forego a hotel stay, ensuring that they would be comfortable at Tía Cristina's house. I hoped these sleeping arrangements didn't feel as strained as they looked. *Go with the flow,* I reminded myself. And so, my second adventure began.

* * *

What would a stay in my birth family's home be without waking up to the clatter of Tía Marcela's cleaning routine? I went downstairs and saw my grandma, *Nonita,* was making *arepas* and she gave me some with scrambled eggs. After breakfast, I made my way back upstairs to my room. I skipped this morning's shower, since no one offered me boiling water. I didn't want to make a special request for fear that I would be seen as a spoiled American, so I shrugged it off and went the day without bathing.

Back home, I had designated a corner of my bedroom to all the gifts I wanted to bring for my birth family. The pile grew over time, eventually creating a laughable struggle of balancing and juggling and tripping over boxes when it came time to pack them into my suitcase. I had worked at Victoria's Secret over the summer, and part of my employee loot from that job included an unopened gift set of lotions and spritzers that I had promised to Tía Cristina. She lit up with gratitude when I handed her the set - and my suitcase breathed a sigh of relief as its load lightened.

Antonio asked me if I wanted to ride with him to drop off my cousin Felipe at his soccer game. Excited to get out into the city and see my recently licensed cousin drive, I hopped in his car. It felt so good to be back in Bogotá! After the quick errand, we were right back at the house. We were greeted by my birth mother, Vincente, *Nonito*, and Sara, who handed me a gift bag with a large stuffed dog inside. This was the second dog-themed present my birth family had given me. During my first visit, my birth mom gave me a "Perfect Petzzz" dog designed to look like it was breathing. I wasn't sure what conclusion they had drawn about me and dogs. I had dogs back home, but I wouldn't consider myself an obsessive dog lover. Our cultural misperceptions and miscommunications had started to feel more amusing than frustrating by then.

It was time to give Sara her gifts—pink Converse shoes (just like mine), hair bows, pencils, erasers, a notepad and a book that served as an emotional lighthouse to me when I was a child. The book is called "Hablo Espanol." Growing up, it helped connect my brothers and I to our Spanish-speaking roots. Written in Spanish with English translations underneath, these pages symbolized the duality of my identity. I wrote a note to Sara inside the front cover. The note was written in English in order to motivate her to learn the language.

With each passing hour, the house became more saturated with people. Sara and I happily played with her new pencils and notepad until I was asked to go with my uncle to move his giant semi-truck from one location to another. The ride itself was terrifying, considering Colombians' fearless disregard for traffic laws. In addition, the only seatbelt available to me had no interest in holding anything down voluntarily, and so I forcefully held it across my chest, mostly to avoid police attention. Not that they seemed to mind all of the other multitude of laws being ignored by practically every car in sight. We moved the truck from a swiss-cheese asphalt lot to another, filthier location. I gripped the worn leather of my seat in an attempt to hold myself down as we bounced around the cabin. I was brought back to the house without a clue as to the point of that errand. Per usual here, I never knew or understood what was going on. That was more liberating than I had allowed myself to realize at the time.

Once I was back at the house, I piled onto *Nonita*'s bed with Santiago, José and Sara. The four of us watched Spiderman until coziness got the best of us and we all drifted off into a family nap. The simple act of peacefully resting alongside my siblings and my cousin brought me a serenity I had only dreamed about. I would remember this tranquility when I needed the strength to deal with the ever-frustrating language barrier. My first trip to Colombia was brimming with adrenaline and curiosity, so although the lack of communication was apparent, it often faded into the background. This time, I found myself even more frustrated with the inability to express myself more deeply. I had become painfully aware of how powerfully communication could alter a group's dynamic. I was intrigued to see how that dynamic would shift when my parents arrived.

Meanwhile, the social dance of gift-giving continued. My birth family gifted me an authentic Colombian hat from my Tío Fidel. *Tío Fidel.* I mentally jotted down the newest addition to my ongoing list of family names. Tío Fidel was perched on the couch downstairs. In my normal routine of introductions, I wrapped my arms around him for a quick hug. Our conversation was taxed by the language barrier until he mentioned the *fiesta* (party) for my parents' arrival. I conveyed a polite display of excitement before the dialogue returned to its awkward pace. A loud chirp rang from his pocket. *Thank God.* His ringing phone broke the bumbling exchange, giving me enough time to sneak off to the kitchen and confirm with my *Nonita* that this was indeed the same Tío who had given me the hat. Finding out I was right, I ran back to give my newly discovered uncle an enthusiastic *gracias.* I may have been struggling to speak Spanish, but I was mastering the art of giving unspoken thanks.

I made my way upstairs to take a shower. To my surprise, the days of bucket showering were gone and upgrades had been made to include what I thought was hot running water. But when the tepid droplets fell onto my skin, they sent a rippling shiver down my spine. If competitive speed showering were a thing, I could have earned myself an Olympic medal.

After my speed-shower, it was time to enact a tradition that seems to exist in almost every culture: "girls' day". I was meant to spend the day with my birth mom and Sara, bonding in a way only a girls' day can provide. While I felt obligated to show excitement, I felt surprisingly uncomfortable. I could feel myself continuing to put distance between my birth mother and me. And yet, the depth of my connection with my adoptive mother is singular. It was unfair to compare the relationships I have with both of my mothers, and yet I would do so compulsively. Logically, I understood that it was healthier to acknowledge the distinct ways both of these women shaped my life. I decided to make more of an effort to bond with my birth mother and accept our relationship as it was, rather than focusing on what I thought it should be. Our relationship was not a threat to what my mother and I shared, and it was time for me to recognize that.

And after all of that talking myself up, girls' day never happened. I depend on the rallying cry of *"¡Vamos!"* ("Let's go!") as a cue that I'm about to be shepherded somewhere for some reason. This particular *¡Vamos!* did not result in the anticipated girls' day. Instead, my day was spent downtown with Antonio and his girlfriend, Galena. We shuffled with the masses into el Transmilenio, Bogotá's public transit system. The cherry-red train cars ferried us into the heart of Bogotá. The thrill of venturing out in the city was soon replaced with the pain of blistered feet. It was my fault for wearing high-heeled wedges in an effort to match Colombian women's style. After a pit stop to acquire much needed bandages for my ankles, we were back at it as fearless explorers. We stopped at a famous little restaurant called La Puerta Falsa where Antonio ordered three *chocolates típicos* (traditional hot chocolate). The server brought us our *tasas* (mugs), which were plated with bread and a block of cheese. I watched in confusion as Antonio and Galena began shredding their cheese into the hot chocolate. Antonio urged me to do the same, and so mind open and curiosity high, I did. And, good gracious, was it delicious! The delights of this excursion were amplified by the fact that we spoke in English for most of the time. The day had proved to be more comforting, adventurous, and relaxing than any girls' day.

* * *

Spending the day speaking broken English with Antonio and Galena sparked an idea. I asked them if they would translate a conversation between my birth mother and me. I had made my decision I needed to ask her about my birth father. They agreed to help. Once we got back to the house, I anxiously crept up to my birth mother with Antonio by my side, ready to unearth the mysteries about the other source of my DNA. Disappointment overcame me as she refused to disclose information with a family member present. I had to find a translator outside of our gene pool in order to unlock these deeply buried secrets. All of the anxiety and expectation that had surfaced over the last few days deflated into defeat. She said that she hoped I was not upset. I lied through my teeth and assured her that I understood.

This was clearly not my day. Shortly after rejecting our conversation about my birth father, she informed me that Tío Fidel would be sleeping in my bedroom that night. What do you get when you combine two twin beds, an exhausted foreigner and a snoring uncle? I'll tell you, you get me calling it an early night and sneaking away upstairs to catch some elusive alone time to journal before bed. I did my best to remain grateful even though the night was heavy in disappointment.

A long night of light sleep left me feeling groggy the next morning. At least I had started to understand my family's rhythms and routines. I stumbled downstairs, half awake, when my birth mother informed me that I was going to the shoe store with Tío Pepe after lunch. What I used to perceive as spontaneous chaos was more intentional than I had realized. Like clockwork, *Nonita* would cook meals for family members who worked at the shoe store. Tío Pepe would come home for lunch, eat his meal, and bring the food *Nonita* had cooked back to the store to give the others. I had begun understanding those sequences and my place in them.

I brought my laptop to the kitchen table and surfed the web while waiting for Tío Pepe to arrive. I would soon find out that I was sitting in his designated seat at the table. Maybe I don't know all of the rhythms and routines quite yet. He walked over to the chair where I was sitting and cleared his throat. I quickly scooted one chair over, hoping I hadn't overstepped my boundaries. We enjoyed lunch together, then were off to the store. In the car, I explained to Tío Pepe that my parents were looking to hire a professional translator during their visit. "Antonio can help. He's very good with English," he reassured me about his son. "Antonio's English is very good, but they need someone fluent," I kindly insisted. He didn't seem to agree. Sure, my parents would benefit from a third-party translator, but I had an underlying motive. I needed someone outside of the family to help me get to the bottom of the story about my birth father. Once we were at the shoe store, I reiterated my desire to hire a translator to both Antonio and Tía Cristina, but both seemed to share Tío Pepe's skepticism.

Why was my family so resistant to hiring a translator? Were they ashamed to reveal the story of my adoption to a stranger? Were they suspicious of letting a stranger into their home? It didn't matter either way. My needs felt abandoned. I felt like I was on an emotional island. My family spent their days talking, connecting, and communicating freely, while I wade through staccato words and clunky phrasing. I was concerned that my parents would encounter the same frustrations without the help of a translator. I feared that I would never know anything about my birth father. The tears welled up in the corner of my eyes, but I used my breath to beg them to quietly back down.

The frustration I felt about the translator was yanked out of my body when my birth mom grabbed my hand and told me to come with her. Like a rag doll, I was pulled in every direction while she quickly uttered *"Le presento a mi hija"* ("I'd like to introduce you to my daughter") to what felt like every human in sight. Most of these people had bought lunches from her earlier in the day and were paying her for them then. With every introduction, I painted a giant smile across my face in the hopes that they wouldn't flood me with questions in Spanish. One resounding theme from these conversations was how similar María and I looked. In a spiritual way, this was a dream come true. I always wanted to look like someone in my family. In an admittedly shallow way, this was a bit offensive. After all, she responded to being called *gordita* (Colombian slang for "chubby girl") because it was plainly obvious she didn't take care of herself physically. I did my best to wipe away the superficial judgments and acknowledge how special it was to share features with a blood relative. Before I could get too lost in thought, I felt a tug on my arm accompanied by the infamous *¡Vamos!* We were off to our next destination, wherever that would be.

After a refreshing stop at the hair salon, María and I jumped into a taxi and headed to Tía Cristina's house. The door flung open as soon as we arrived, revealing Sara's boisterous but petite frame behind it. She yanked me inside. My arm experienced *déjà vu* as she pulled me around from place to place and refused to release me. There was no doubt from whom she had learned this. After a bout of giggling, playing, and teaching the English words for different colors to Sara, I went upstairs to my room. My parents were set to arrive the next day. I could feel my stomach clench as the anxiety crept in. There was no doubt that their arrival would shift the dynamics with my birth family. I had spent practically all of my life fantasizing about one day meeting my birth mother, and then introducing her to my parents. For so many years, I had run through every possible circumstance and outcome of that meeting.

That fantasy was about to become a reality. *When I open my eyes, they'll almost be here*, I thought. And somehow, my eyes grew heavy enough to outweigh the rapid beating of my heart, and off to sleep I drifted.

CHAPTER ELEVEN
Meeting

A single ray of sun shone through a crack in the blinds. My eyes shot open. The day had come. I pulled in every bit of air I could sweep into my lungs as my heart raced expectantly. The family that created me and the family that shaped me would soon be in the same house. And my life would be forever changed as a consequence. The idea of my two identities uniting almost sent me into an existential spiral until I heard *Nonita*'s symphony of *clangs* and *clongs* in the kitchen. I meandered downstairs with a question for *Nonita* burning at the tip of my tongue.

"Are you happy?" I asked her. The combination of her mumbled Spanish and the thickness of her accent often made it difficult for us to communicate, yet our spirits seemed to talk freely regardless. Any time her sun-spotted hands caressed my cheek, a smile would light the sweet wrinkles of her face and I could feel her love warming me from the inside out. She replied with a simple, *"Si,"* and returned the question. After I assured her I was, we shared a moment that would impress upon me forever. We told each other we loved one another with all our hearts. Following this, she blessed me with the sign of the cross, something she had done since the first time I met her (especially any time before leaving the house). We laughed as she taught me how to complete the blessing motion myself. Her love left me beaming. I felt confident that the day would unfold beautifully.

My optimism was put on hold when I couldn't reach my parents. I had emailed them the night before informing them that I couldn't secure a translator, that we would be doing some traveling while they were here to another city called Guadalupe, and about the tight rooming situation. Hopefully they were still excited to come. My mind listed all of the possible reasons for their radio silence. As my nervous energy reached its height, I heard the digital ding I needed to hear. My mom had responded to one of my messages with, "Don't worry, city lips." Laughter flung out of my mouth. *Thank you for breaking my tension, mom.* She had recently ordered a lip plumper called "City Lips" which had quickly turned into an inside joke. The plumper made my already full lips even more dramatic, which was not the case for my mom's "paper cut lips," as she referred to them. This message dissolved my anxiety in a way only she had the power to do.

My parents would not arrive until 9:30 p.m., which made the day feel like an eternity. My mind used the additional free time to construct some more worries. I seemed to have a knack for doing that. The night before, I had shared some of the complex feelings I was experiencing with my friends on the "Adopted from Colombia" Facebook page. I mentioned that my birth mother told me she wanted to hold up a sign at the airport that read, "Thank you for bringing up my daughter." *Your daughter?* Puzzling signage, to be sure. It made more sense to me that my parents might say, "Thank you for giving our daughter life." The confusing logistics paired with my sensitivity toward the issue made for a complex mix. My Facebook family reassured me that my feelings and reactions were par for the course considering my situation. My peers also advised that I stop resisting my birth mother (something my mom had long before insisted I do). Being adopted, I was always asked if I knew who my "real" mom was. Every hard chapter, beautiful beginning, lesson and memory was created and guided by my mother in America. Whether she adopted me had nothing to do with her degree of "realness". She was a "real" mother in every way a mother can be. Being a birth parent doesn't automatically mean you tag on "real" to their title. The frustration tightened around my mind like a girdle. I found myself more and more upset. I tried to dissect why I couldn't accept María the way I wanted - or needed - to. The stark differences between my two mothers was ever-present in my mind. My mom had a natural ability to safeguard my emotional health, something my birth mother was never able to do. On the other hand, my birth mom was most concerned with making sure my basic physical needs were met. I pondered if this was cultural. My birth mother was always tending to my belly, making sure it stayed full. Perhaps that was the way she knew how to demonstrate her maternal love for me. I did my best to drop my mounting frustrations and embrace the experience to come. Watching my sweet little sister play with the stencil set I gave her helped ease my overworked mind. Her ability to plant carefree joy wherever she goes snapped me back to the present. And my present was certainly worthy of appreciation. My two families were on the cusp of weaving together in a way that felt like a dream.

Time moved like taffy as I waited to go to the airport to pick up my parents. My routine of restless pacing was interrupted when my birth mom arrived at the house with a stunning flower arrangement. Not only was the display one of the most breathtaking I had ever seen, but it also exuded my birth mother's gratitude. Attached to the flowers read a small note, "Thank you for raising my daughter. I hope you have a wonderful time in Colombia. God bless you." The sincerity behind her appreciation diffused any of my lingering resentment. I knew my parents were the type of people who would receive these flowers graciously and understand the significance behind them.

* * *

Antonio, Sara and my birth mom finally loaded into the car to go to the airport and welcome my parents to their Colombian adventure. I was surprised that more people didn't join us, but ultimately, I knew it was better that way. The impending moment warranted intimacy. On the ride to the airport, I sat in the front seat while Antonio drove. My birth mom and Sara took the backseat. I stretched my hand back to hold Sara's. I could feel my birth mom's quiet tension, so I reached my other hand back and found hers. I sat there, connected to two of the most pivotal people in this chapter of my life. We gripped one another, sharing the same quick pulse.

We parked at the airport and made our way inside. We scanned the dense crowd looking for my parents. Once I caught a glimpse of them, I reached for my camera so I could record the special moment when my two worlds would merge. In perfect gringo fashion, they waved excitedly through the glass at us while flashing ear-to-ear smiles. While we waited for them to go through another line, I noted my birth mother's behavior. She was smiling quietly. When they reached us, my parents went straight for her, enveloping her in an emotional hug. My dad repeated, *"Gracias, María"* over and over while tears flowed from each of their eyes. The connection was instantaneous. I stood back to watch the three of them interact. Their tearful embraces touched my heart, but not enough to make me cry in solidarity. I felt like an emotionless statue again, which I was growing used to.

We loaded into the car to make our way back to the house. This time, my parents and I took the backseat. Sara sat on my lap. Antonio drove, while María was in the front seat. My parents quickly caught on to the connection between Sara and me. They marveled at how much we look alike, referring to her as my "mini-me." Once we arrived at the house, my parents were given the grand tour. They were visibly impressed. They briefly met *Nonita* who bashfully uttered a quick hello, half-asleep, before ducking back into bed. My parents marveled at how beautiful *Nonita* was. I felt proud to show her off to them. Her spirit paired with her all-knowing smile made for a type of beauty that is not easily described.

My birth mom summoned us to the kitchen to eat the sandwiches she had made for us. Sara plopped onto her favorite seat--my lap. My mom and Sara engaged in playful exchanges and imitation games. Their sweet interactions transcended any language barriers. If I would have been told that one day I would be in Bogotá, Colombia, with my parents, my birth mother, and my half-sister, I would never have believed it. Life has a way of keeping you humble. You never do know what's around the bend of your own path.

Being with my parents in Bogotá cemented my whirlwind experiences as unquestionably real. My first trip felt like a hazy, surreal dream. I sometimes wondered if I had imagined the whole thing. Nostalgia was lonesome. I relived moments by myself. Memories circled in my head in solitude. There was no one with whom I could reminisce. Trying to explain my experience made me feel like a being from a distant planet trying to interact with unaware earthlings. I had grown preemptively excited about all the reminiscing I would do with my parents one day. And, finally, that day had come. We could now revel in the observations and experiences from our distant planet. With this realization came a new wave of gratitude. This opportunity I had been given was both rare and beautiful. And then there was relief brought on by the fact that I could speak fluid English with my parents. We spoke freely about my birth mother. Their appreciation for her elevated my own. Positivity wrapped around us as we smiled, talked, and prepared for the following day of sightseeing and family meeting.

Initially, the plan was to bring my parents downtown with Antonio and Galena, but a soccer match between Argentina and Colombia diverted our plans. We decided to reschedule to a day when we could take the time to wander freely around the city with no time constraints. In honor of the game, I donned the Colombian soccer jersey gifted to me during my first trip. I dreaded disappointing my parents with the change of plans, but they long ago mastered going with the flow. They were ready to participate in any adventure coming their way. I wondered if they would want to venture out on their own, as I had an itch to do so myself.

Getting ready for the day, per usual, meant becoming a temporary human icicle in the shower. To add to my own discomfort, I made the foolish decision to shave my legs. The combination of cold water, goosebumps and a sharp razor resulted in irritated skin. I showed Tía Cristina to see if she had any creams or lotions to soothe my angered legs. She went outside to her garden, cut off an aloe leaf, split it open and rubbed it straight on my legs. The aloe immediately calmed my speckled skin. I was in awe of her resourcefulness.

On my first trip, I found nothing funny about the frigid showers. But with my parents there, it became a running joke. They dreaded jumping in the cold water, but their dread came with laughter. Having them around helped me find the humor in everything. After we had briskly showered and gotten ready, we went downstairs for a breakfast of *arepas* with eggs and soup. I nonchalantly observed my parents, curious how they would handle the same scenarios I found myself in during my first visit. My mom slyly scooped some of her food onto my dad's plate, nervous that it would be seen as rude if she didn't finish the meal. I smiled. I was more than familiar with the cultural obstacle course they were now navigating.

After breakfast, we all went upstairs so my parents could give my family the gifts they had brought from the States. Who doesn't like to start a day with gifts? This would set the tone for the day. My mom, who was practically a professional gift giver, presented Sara with a Disney princess coloring book, a pack of crayons, and a Cinderella Barbie doll. Sara bubbled over with excitement in only the way Sara can. My mom also brought *Nonita* and my birth mom scarves, Burt's Bees beauty products, and some signature Southern snacks. They were tickled by the quintessentially Georgian smorgasbord of peaches, pecans, roasted peanuts and cookies.

My eyes darted to the corner of the room and spotted a heap of gift bags. Clearly, my parents had thought of everyone. Tío Fidel and his wife would receive their gifts when we visited them in Guadalupe the next day.

After our impromptu Christmas, we walked with Antonio to the family shoe store. My hairs were standing on end and my eyes scanning left and right. I was far more protective of my parents than I had anticipated. With their light skin, European features, and American clothing, they stood out like sore thumbs. Antonio and I translated for them at the shoe store. They became a spectacle for everyone around, including Santiago. As our day continued, I noticed my aunt and my mom walking arm in arm while Antonio and my dad walked side by side in conversation. The effortless communion between my two families was proving to be stronger than language barriers and cultural differences.

As we were walking, a taxi pulled up next to us honking wildly. It was Vincente, by pure coincidence. The universe had pushed our paths to merge at that perfect moment in Bogotá. He reached through the window to shake my parents' hands, assuring them that we would all spend time together later. We moseyed on and did a little shopping for my brothers back in the United States. We found some knockoff Colombian soccer jerseys being sold by a street vendor. They definitely weren't authentic jerseys, which in my opinion, made them even more authentically Colombian.

We made our way back to the house eventually, choosing to abandon our plans to learn more about my birth family instead. María and *Nonita* explained to my parents how my grandma raised all seven kids by herself. *Nonita* described how she would wake up every morning at 3 a.m. in order to get everything prepared in time to get them all to school. Our conversation cleared up some of the details I was fuzzy about, such as the birth order of my *tías* and *tíos*. The oldest was Tío Oscar, followed by Jaime, Natalia, María, Fidel, Cristina and Cesar. The pieces of this familial puzzle continued to come together as time went on.

* * *

A considerable amount of time spent in Colombia is centered around food. During this particular lunch, we ate a traditional soup called *ajiaco* made by my birth mom. My parents very clearly enjoyed every slurping spoonful. As our bowls emptied, Sara joined us to color in the new book my parents had given her. The dynamics felt surprisingly natural. I realized that my parents were the missing ingredients to make this family recipe feel complete. We sat on the sofa and joined together in song. We sang nursery rhymes to Sara as she beamed back at us and danced around. The energy and newness of the day was as exhilarating as it was exhausting, and my dad was the first to go down, knocked out cold on the couch.

My mom and I hoped for our own cat nap, but before our eyes could shut Tío Cesar burst through the door with an exuberant *"Hola!"* that jolted us to our feet for another round of joyful introductions. I flexed my translating muscle as I introduced Tío Cesar to my parents. He chatted excitedly about his trucking job and raved about the apple of his eye-- the family parrot, Rebecca. Rebecca had established a pretty hostile reputation with everyone. Everyone other than Tío Cesar, apparently. Committed to proving that she would never bite him, Cesar waved for all of us to follow him downstairs to watch him give her a kiss on the beak. It didn't surprise me in the least when my mom decided to pet Rebecca. My mom and Tío Cesar must share a similar energy, because Rebecca did not mind her affection one bit. She even allowed my mom to put her face near the cage. Following in my mom's footsteps, I let Rebecca sit on my hand. My bravery lasted a whopping 30 seconds before I panicked and gently shooed the bird away.

We went back to the kitchen to chat over a round of sweets. Our dialogue veered toward visas and passports. My birth mom, Santiago, Vincente, and Sara wanted to visit the United States. My mom insinuated that she might cover their expenses, but the weight of that pressure felt like an anchor landing in my gut. That was putting too much expectation on my parents. We jotted down some basic information, leaving me concerned about where this exchange would lead. What would it feel like to insert my birth family into my American reality?

CHAPTER TWELVE
Sightseeing

The following day we would embark on the Guadalupe portion of our adventure. With my birth mom already on the long bus ride there, it was my temporary responsibility to care for Sara. She would ride up with us with Tío Pepe behind the wheel. Logistically, it made the most sense for Sara to spend the night in my bed so I could keep an eye on her. Emotionally, it scratched an itch I didn't know I had. We cuddled up together for a moment that would stick in my memory like a snowflake on ice. I was having my first sleepover with my little sister. I did my best to cherish every precious second until I involuntarily drifted off to sleep.

When my eyes peeled open the next morning, I was greeted by Sara's toothy grin shining down on me. She gently caressed my face with her tiny hand. I could sense her imprinting every detail. Once I was properly awake, we quietly laid side by side. There is a singular comfort in sharing silence with your family. After a few minutes had passed, she whispered that I was beautiful as she leaned to kiss me on the head. If only all of my mornings could begin with that much unconditional love. The house was soon buzzing as our little troop of travelers got ready, ate breakfast, and hit the road by 8 a.m.

We certainly felt every minute of the six-hour ride to Guadalupe. Tío Pepe drove with my dad beside him in the passenger seat. Antonio, my mom and I squashed ourselves into the backseat. Sara played a game of musical chairs on our laps. Admittedly, I am accustomed to a certain degree of comfort as an American. Car rides like these reminded me of just how privileged I was. Nonetheless, I kept my mouth shut. If a five-year-old could hang in there with no complaints, then so could I. We watched the rolling landscapes and small-towns peep in and out of view as we made our way to Guadalupe.

We arrived at Tío Fidel's house by early afternoon and celebrated in true Colombian fashion--by eating. We were joined by Tía Natalia, who also lived in Guadalupe. She marched to a different beat than the rest of our clan. I learned that she was considered the black sheep of the family, something that had become apparent through the many awkward stalls that littered our conversations. Regardless, Tía Natalia proudly guided us around her city, offering plenty of inside scoops into Guadalupe. I wondered whether my birth mother had stayed at the house because of the walking distance or because she refused to spend time with her sister. From what I had gathered, the tension between Tía Natalia and the rest of the family peaked when she refused to contribute her share for *Nonito*'s medical bills. In Colombia, providing care for your parents is more than a moral issue, it's a legal one. Antonio had shared that once parents reach a certain age, it becomes their child's responsibility to care for them and their needs. The culture embraces a deep respect for elders and places an emphasis on family responsibility. I wondered...why was she the only sibling that wouldn't help in a medical crisis? I knew the issue had reached the courts at one point, but I chose to overlook that conflict and enjoy the day I was having with her. Tía Natalia deserved a clean slate with me, and I deserved the opportunity to come to my own conclusions. And we all deserved a day without tension.

Natalia's daughter, Ivette, joined us as we explored Guadalupe. Tucked into lush mountains, the town felt like it was being guarded by nature. Rows of palm trees marked the area apart from the wild, untamed landscapes that surround it. We peeked around a couple of schools and churches in the village, and even stumbled upon a festival in the park. Our trek through the tiny town eventually landed us at the cemetery. Ivette explained how beautiful she thought it was. My head tilted. I tried to see the beauty she was seeing. My eyes couldn't focus on anything other than the towering gates and barbed wire meant to protect the dead and their treasures from thieves.

Our exploration continued as beads of sweat streamed down my back. The combination of heat and humidity felt different in this rural tropic. I looked on in loathing at my long jeans. In a moment of oven-baked desperation, I had actually considered cutting my pants into shorts. I scanned the streets.

Nearly everyone was comfortably wearing long pants. Happily, even. I needed to acclimate--both my body temperature and my attitude.

The air finally cooled as the sun ducked behind a silhouette of mountaintops. We decided to revisit the festival. More townspeople had gathered, bringing with them more atmosphere. The celebrations amplified when a group of men arrived on horseback. The riders were laughing, yelling, and taking shots of *aguardiente* as their horses kicked and bucked wildly. Stone cold sober, I hid from the careless hoopla and crossed my fingers for everyone's safety. Before worry could consume me, I saw a donkey strut carelessly down the street, completely unbothered by the gathering. At one point, the donkey paused, looked around, and began chewing on the mirror of a motorcycle parked outside of a bar. I laughed to myself and took a picture. That was a moment I wouldn't want to forget.

After a festive evening, we made our way back to the house to plop our worn bodies on the couch and watch television. One of my cousins turned to a channel where a man was doing stand-up comedy (in Spanish of course). Every punchline resulted in my birth family erupting in laughter while we, the English-speaking Americans, exchanged clueless glances. I didn't mind not understanding. I loved hearing them laugh. I laid my head on my mom's lap. Nervous that my birth mother was feeling jealous, I followed her when she wandered outside to the balcony. My anxiety melted away as she wrapped her arms around me and told me she loved me. "I love you, too." We expressed our gratitude for one another and all that had taken place. She thanked me for searching for her. Involuntarily, my arms squeezed tighter and tighter around her. In that single moment, our bond became as tight as that hug on the balcony overlooking little Guadalupe.

While I hoped the tenderness of that moment would rock me sweetly to sleep that night, I had no such luck. The stale heat wrapped around every inch of my skin and my pores were smothered with sweat. I tossed. I turned. My uncle Fidel may be comfortable living without air conditioning, but I certainly wasn't. I even optimistically, perhaps naively, cracked the window in hopes that a rush of unexpected cool air would surprise me and find its way to my room. I imagined undressing the heat from my body and began to feel the gentle drift that could only mean sleep. Unfortunately, the heat wasn't my only obstacle. The loud music at the festival brought the party that I *thought* I left, right to my room. And closing the window was not an option. I would have to welcome the party music as my lullaby. Luckily, at some point in the wee hours, my body surrendered and agreed to the given circumstances. I finally fell asleep. But after some much-needed rest, I awoke and couldn't believe my ears. The morning sun was shining, the birds were chirping, and the festival music was *still* playing. Do these people ever sleep?

* * *

In the morning, my parents came to me asking for my help with translating to my uncle that they needed towels to take a shower. Unsure that I would be able to translate accurately, I asked Antonio for his assistance. I was surprised when he told me that we were expected to bring our own towels with us. I told him that it's normal in the United States for the host to offer the guest towels to use during their stay. According to him, that's not how it works here in Colombia. I had already been met with surprising shower expectations back in Bogotá when my aunt Cristina asked where my *chanclas* (flip-flops) were prior to showering. Apparently, it's common to use them in the shower here but since I was unaware of that, she let me borrow hers. Thankfully, Antonio was just as understanding of the cultural differences as she was and helped my parent's and I in the task of retrieving towels to use during our stay in Guadalupe.

Surrounded by an endless fog of heat, I was pleasantly surprised to hear we would be going to swim at a pool today. My cousins and I piled into the bed of my uncle's truck and cut through an Amazonian jungle to get there. Most pools I had swam in before shared a common element: you could see through to the bottom. That was not the case this time. Eager to escape the heat, I submerged myself into the murky water.

After a quick dip, I cracked open a beer and watched the kids as they splashed happily in the pool. As if the scene wasn't striking enough, a white horse happened to roam by us. She majestically greeted us with a neigh as she trotted off into the mountainous horizon. *Is this real life or am I in a post card?*

At lunchtime, we gathered under a covered terrace sipping beer and eating a huge spread of food. The heat from the sun combined with the scenic view made for a joyous, relaxed atmosphere. The beers didn't hurt either. My birth mother abstained from drinking. *Interesting.* Another note I would add to my mental list of her idiosyncrasies. Sitting back and watching my parents blissfully sip their beers as they sat aside my birth mom sent a ripple of gratitude through my heart. We didn't say much but our smiles said enough. We soaked in the mountain landscape together and listened to the laughter echoing off the terrace walls as the kids played on billiard tables behind us. The energy was that of pure joy. I could have stayed there forever. Once we returned to the house, I took a nap outside on the balcony floor with Santiago. The cool tiles of the floor chilled our burned, tired skin. The simple pleasure of cold tiles on my warm back was all I needed in that moment. Having my biological brother nap beside me was the icing on top of the cake.

After napping, I took a longer shower than usual. For the first time, I welcomed the cold water. My burned skin felt relief with every cold drop. When I was done, I got ready to go out with Antonio, Felipe, Ivette, and Santiago. The energy shifted as everyone felt a sense of relief after breaking away from our elders. As we passed the park, we saw the silhouettes of people dancing and celebrating and heard the children shrieking as they played carnival games. We spent a while walking around the festival and eventually parked ourselves on a bench. My cousins and brother were somehow teeming with energy. The sun had drained me of mine. I called it a night and began making my way back to the house...when I felt a twinge of fear. I was alone. It was dark. This setup never panned out well in movies. I reminded myself that I was neither in Bogotá nor Atlanta, but instead in a quaint, idyllic town tucked into the Colombian countryside. I shook off my concerns, took a deep breath and smiled knowing the fun my cousins were likely having. Their bond was strong. While partying was part of their routine, taking care of their family and contributing through hard work always came first. I also learned one essential rule: what happens among cousins, stays among cousins. Lucky for them, I am a walking vault.

The following day, Tío Pepe, Antonio, my parents, and I drove three hours to a national park referred to as "Panache" (properly called Parque Nacional del Chicamocha) to explore the Colombia's famed natural beauty. The car danced around the winding mountain roads leaving me with a dizzying case of motion sickness. Coupled with my menstrual cramps, I was not a very happy camper. After a quick stop to stretch our legs and regroup, we were back on the road. Luckily, I had built up my endurance for long, uncomfortable car rides by this point.

And then we arrived at an overwhelming sight. It took a moment to catch my breath and really take in the splendor. We peered over the vast canyon, with mountains lined up like dominoes, in awe of its enormity. There were no words for the grandeur of this site.

We hopped on a cable car and traveled through the canyon. On the other side, lunch awaited us. After we satiated our bellies, we explored a little more. We met some surprisingly terrifying ostriches at an ostrich farm, made wishes at a fountain, took pictures with a huge monument, and checked out some native artifacts. Our field trip to Panache was enjoyable and successful, but we were tired and ready to make the winding journey back to the house. That night, I slept like a rock.

I awoke the next morning to a chorus of laughter and loud voices echoing from the kitchen of Tío Fidel's house. Half-awake, I shoved my body toward the commotion to find out what it was all about. As I got closer, I could see my dad putting something in his mouth as my birth family crowded around him and cheered him on. He was a couple of oblivious bites in when I had to tell him he was eating ants. Referred to as *hormigas barrigonas,* these large, pot-bellied ants are a popular snack that time of year. He immediately paused his crunching as his eyes shot wide and his eyebrows launched to the top of his forehead. In an attempt to be polite, he forced the bite down his throat. My own laughter was lost among the chorus of cackles surrounding us. I imagined all the scenarios he could get himself into without me by his side providing rudimentary interpretation. There are some joys a daughter can't put a price tag on. Watching my father unknowingly eat ants surrounded by my blood relatives was worth every cent in airfare. I continued laughing to myself as I went to pack for the long journey back to Bogotá.

CHAPTER THIRTEEN
Reeling

Whatever the car equivalent is to sea legs, I earned them on my round trip to Guadalupe. We finally made it. *Ahhh, back in Bogotá.* Stretching and moving my body outside of the car felt like a humble little blessing. As I physically unwound, I realized I had developed a particular relationship to this place. It felt more like home than before. I also felt distinctly closer to my birth mother. After witnessing the wave of daily challenges her life entails, I made the decision that once I finished school and secured a career for myself, I would send her financial support. I pondered where these funds could be best applied...maybe Sara's medical bills? Or perhaps sending Sara to an English school? I had to curb my expectations knowing that it would probably not amount to that much. I just knew I had to do whatever was within my power. I felt compelled to show gratitude for my birth mother through tangible actions. I was lost in my thoughts about the distant future when I was greeted by a reminder of the present. My journey here would soon come full circle. On Wednesday, my birth mother, my parents, and I were scheduled to visit FANA. I knew that stepping foot into the place from which I had been adopted would split my reality in two. I would soon stand in the place that once defined my future and now held the key to my past. Excitement, and a rush of anxiety, tingled across my skin.

No sooner had I contemplated paying some of Sara's medical bills, the poor little one came down with the chicken pox. Her misery continued for three days until we made the decision to take her to the doctor. My parents and I decided we would shoulder the cost and lift that burden off my birth family. A decision like this one would likely be a weighty one for them, but for us it resulted in around $50 U.S. dollars. This was a small sacrifice for ensuring Sara's health.

Her body, especially her kidneys, had been put through way too much for the limited years she had been on earth. Antonio enlightened us on the struggles she had already so bravely endured. He had shared that, right after Sara was born, María was hospitalized. I couldn't translate what exactly made her sick. What I did catch was that baby Sara spent this time with Tía Cristina, Tío Pepe, Antonio and Felipe. It was during this difficult chapter that the bond between Tío Pepe and Sara solidified. To this day, he is like her second father. Antonio also grew close to Sara. He would often care for her when my birth mother was away at work. Both he and my Tía Cristina were naturally strict with her. They were comfortable providing her with the boundaries she was missing. I could see how this dynamic played out during my time in Colombia. If Antonio asked Sara to do something, she responded immediately. If Santiago, Vincente or my birth mother asked her, the lag time was pretty obvious, and sometimes, pretty comical.

The rhythms of Bogotá felt perfectly in tune: the Colombian soccer team battled it out against Peru on TV. The men at the house yelled at the television every time Peru scored a goal. María insisted we visit the hair salon and my mom and I happily joined her on this indulgent excursion. We looked forward to having clean and styled hair as well as polished nails. Making this pampering a ritual part of life was genius on their part. Reality in Colombia was raw and demanding and the relief this self-care provided was essential. I had grown accustomed to it and wondered how I could make it a part of my life back in the States. My mom and I decided to pay for my birth mom's salon services, but she surprised us by getting nothing done. My parents and I had found a particular brand of joy in giving back to the family that made me. We decided not to question her refusal out of fear of coming across as rude. Instead, we focused on savoring this sacred bonding time between the three of us. Looks like I had my "girls' day" after all, and I couldn't have asked for a better one. Our bonding continued once we got back to the house. The vibe was enjoyable and relaxed. The natural cadence of our day brought ease to my often overwrought mind. After a few meandering conversations, my birth mom, Santiago, Sara, and Vincente headed back to their house.

The energy shifted sharply soon after they left. My parents, Tía Cristina, *Nonita*, Tío Fidel and I dove into a conversation that shook my peace. Tía Cristina shared with me that María was alone when she gave birth to me, and that if they would have known such an important event was transpiring, they would have all been present for the moment I came into the world. As the heaviness of the conversation sank into me like a sack of coffee beans, Tío Fidel abruptly stood and signaled his exit. I could see water flooding his eyes. He was working hard to keep it together. While he intended for his goodnight to be brief so he could escape the overwhelm of emotion, I refused to let him slip away like that. My arms wrapped around him as I poured out my gratitude for how he so generously let my parents and me stay at his house in Guadalupe. Prior to this interaction, I was convinced that he didn't like me all that much. I assumed it was due to my lack of Spanish speaking skills. How naive. Something as simple as language could never touch the depths of love built into this family.

A beat passed after I said goodnight to Tío Fidel. With my heart in my throat, I tried my best to reenter the conversation that continued to flow in the kitchen. Next hefty item on the emotional docket to discuss was my birthday. Tía Cristina shared that before meeting me, my birth mother experienced a sprinkling of depressions throughout her life. Every holiday, whether it was Christmas or a family member's birthday, my birth mother would sneak away to cry in private. No one had ever figured out why festive days made her so somber. One year, while celebrating Tío Pepe's birthday on April 29th, my birth mother emotionally told the family that someone very special to her was born on March 30th. That was my birthday. I could feel the blood pounding in my neck. I had spent every one of my birthdays secretly hoping she was thinking about me. I justified that even if she forgot about me 364 days out of the year, the one day that I was bound to cross her mind was my birthday. I never wanted her to isolate herself and sulk, but her emotional tie to that day brought me such closure. My life had been littered in doubt about whether she even thought of me. Come to find out, our hearts were tethered the whole time.

The conversational roller coaster was far from over. Antonio came home and shed light to more peculiar, and possibly disturbing, elements to the story this family had come to know as truth. He claimed that my birth mother believed I was being raised in London by my wealthy birth father, but then she eventually found out he had put me up for adoption without her consent. I was stunned. I was perplexed. I had followed the hairpin curves of every family story so far, but this didn't make sense to me. I made the decision to stop the conversation. My birth mother had previously requested an interpreter for these kinds of emotional discussions. We solemnly nodded in agreement that this would be the best idea going forward, said goodnight to one another and I peeled away, reeling in confusion.

I made my way upstairs to talk to my parents in private. I needed their calming presence. Before I could begin convincing myself of the story's merit in a spiral of anxiety, my parents swooped in. They assured me that everything I had heard was untrue. That was the first time I had heard anything about my birth mom believing I was in London with my birth father. The more we circled around it, the more I could see how the story had come to be. We guessed that my birth mother had lied to protect herself from the shame of telling everyone that she had put me up for adoption herself. How else did she know what FANA was when I mentioned going there with my parents? Furthermore, how would my adoption papers have her fingerprints and signatures on it? It became increasingly clear why she didn't want a translator related to the family when discussing these details. She would end up tangled in the decades-long lie she had birthed.

The subject matter made the conversation with my parents naturally intense. My inward frustration and discomfort projected outward as rudeness toward my mom. As she left to brush her teeth, we caught eyes and I could see her tears forming. What had I done? Tears welled in my own eyes as I snapped out of my cycle of self-pity. I ran over to my dad, who was sitting quietly on the edge of the bed, and allowed myself to unravel in his arms. He gently reminded me that this experience was just as emotional for them as it was for me. My mom must have heard my meltdown (let's be honest--I'm not a quiet crier) because she zipped back into the room and threw herself next to me. We all laced our arms around one another and let the emotions pour out freely. Crying in unison was the perfect release for the whirlwind of emotions this journey had triggered. We pressed pause on our typical family dynamic and just existed as three, vulnerable and emotionally exhausted human beings. We were each in unchartered territory, but at least we were navigating together. We agreed to hold more patience for another as we continued to forge on in this exploration of the unknown.

* * *

There is an art form that never found its way to the USA: flowing. Every day in Colombia is another lesson in rolling with the punches. The people here do this so gracefully. One particular day would challenge my handle on this practice. We were supposed to call FANA to arrange our visit. After a heavy dose of reflection, I made the decision that I did not want my birth mother there with us. I wanted the visit to be celebratory. After all, for my parents and me, this place represents a high point of our lives. Our family would be born from that place. It was very different for María. Within those walls her family would be torn apart and changed forever. The circumstances I was born into were replaced by a new, very different life.

My decision relieved María. While she put on her best disappointed face, I already knew her expressions too well. That visit would entail experiencing the pain of her past all over again. She told me she only wanted to join because she thought it would make me happy. My life is filled with people who make the best decisions possible in order to bring me happiness. I am not so sure what I did in a past life to warrant so much thoughtfulness and love this go around.

When I told my birth mother that I didn't want her to go to FANA with us, I was certain I had just "flowed" my way out of one very sticky and painful situation. I thought I could handle anything. That was before I tried waxing. Later that day, a woman came to the house to wax my legs, since I refused to shave them in the icy shower. A few days prior I had asked Tía Cristina how she kept her legs so silky smooth. She told me her secret was waxing and took it upon herself to arrange for a woman to come wax me. I had dabbled with eyebrow waxing before, but body waxing was an entirely different animal. As it turned out, using wax to rip the hair out of your body is quite literally the stickiest and most painful experience imaginable. While my armpits and legs were surely never going to be the same, it was a worthwhile experience to see my mom bent over in laughter. In the midst of her laughter she repeated "beauty is pain", a phrase I had heard her say jokingly many times growing up and never stopped rolling my eyes at. However, in this instance, my eyes couldn't do anything except squeeze shut and fill with tears as I felt each hair being ripped from its follicle. I vowed to always and forever respect Colombian women and their unbelievable pain tolerance. Silky, smooth, and tingling legs, I was ready for the day.

Antonio, Tía Cristina, my parents and I headed to my birth mother's house for lunch. We sat down to a presentation of individually wrapped, alluringly deep dishes of lasagna. My eyes must have doubled in size. Next to our dishes was a stack of sandwich bread. I was confused at first, but then it hit me. I had requested bread with my lasagna when she made this meal during my first visit to Colombia. At the time I was hoping for something that resembled the garlic bread I had grown accustomed to eating with my Italian dishes back home. Even though the white sandwich bread was totally different, the intent was precious to me. She remembered. Knowing that she knew some of my favorite foods made it feel even more like she was my mother. It's funny how sliver-sized experiences like this weave together to cement the bond between us. Of course, I hit a setback before I could become too proud of our relationship milestones. I suppose that's how any relationship develops. We had taken one emotional step forward so it was about time for two uncomfortable steps back. Little Sara, still battling chicken pox, was getting ready for another doctor's appointment. This would be a group field trip--as most things there tended to be. We all crammed into Vincente's taxi and made the journey to a part of Bogotá I had never seen. Sara was dressed nicely in a beautiful white dress. I questioned this wardrobe choice but soon realized that going to the doctor for them was the equivalent of going to church. One must be dressed in a way that shows they respect the environment and the people in it. At least that's what I gathered. When we arrived at the medical clinic we went inside and waited in a small waiting room for about twenty minutes. During this time, I entertained Sara with games on my phone but tried not to draw too much attention since I had been warned about showing technology in public. Apparently having a smartphone out in a crowd of people is an easy way to become a target to be robbed. When it was our turn to enter the Doctor's office it was obvious that the Doctor was smitten by Sara. He was very patient with her as she ran around his office and played with the toys that were in there for children's entertainment. I got the vibe that Sara had been going to him for medical exams for much of her life. After he finished with her examination, he was quick to prescribe a soothing ointment to quiet Sara's irritated skin. I waited for the perfect opportunity to jump in and pay for her appointment, but before I could, María handed him a homemade lunch. This interaction certainly seemed like a well-received trade. In return for the lunch, he gave my birth mom a paper prescription for Sara's medicine. I was impressed with my birth mom's strategy of paying for medical visits with food she had prepared. I had a feeling this was an agreement they had done before. After the exchange was made, my birth mom informed us that we needed to go to a nearby pharmacy to pick up the ointment. Thus, we all said our goodbyes to the doctor and made our way back into Vincente's taxi. When we arrived at the pharmacy only my birth mother and I went inside while the rest of our crew waited in the car. I stood next to my birth mom at the counter while she interacted with the pharmacy employee. When it was time to pay, I reached my hand in my pocket to pull out the money my parents had given me which was originally designated for the doctor's appointment. Since María had already taken care of that with her homemade meal, I was ready to pay for the medicine instead. With my money-filled hand already extended, I transitioned my offer and agreed to pay for Sara's prescriptions. Without missing a beat, my birth mother tried to quickly add an expensive sunscreen to our purchase. Taken aback, I counted out my money to show her it wouldn't be enough for the additional sunscreen. María's disappointment was palpable. I felt myself become concerned that she might be taking advantage of my kindness.

This disappointment became the impetus for the negative feelings I was doing my best not to acknowledge. I had noticed whenever my birth mom received a compliment from me or my parents, it would become a recurring theme for the day. She would continuously find opportunities to fish for more compliments. At one point she was bold enough to say to my parents, "People tell me I make beautiful children." Then came the exaggerated pause. She was clearly waiting for my parents to agree with her. I focused my eyes forward but inside they were rolling around relentlessly. Stewing in these negative emotions proved oddly satisfying. I stayed cozy in my stew until a realization washed upon me: my resentment might stem from the fact that my birth mother is a different person than who I had spent most of my life imagining her to be. In my fantasies, my birth mother would one day become deeply woven into my American life. It seems I had grown emotionally invested in who I thought she would be. My mind had always painted her as a gorgeous and successful Colombian woman. Instead, reality brought me an overweight and impoverished woman dependent on others to get by in life. But she is so much more than that. She has an extraordinary ability to make quick friendships. She is a cunning negotiator and finds clever ways to barter for what she and her family needs to survive. If anything, she's resourceful. And wasn't the most important thing that my birth mother wanted to meet me, get to know me, and connect with me? Still, I found myself harboring tumultuous feelings about the dynamics of our relationship. On top of that, I felt myself pushing my parents away. I was trying to be kind to myself and every character in my elaborately blended family, but my mixed emotions were swirling into an uncomfortable concoction that sat heavy in my stomach.

When we got back to Tía Cristina's house I went to the restroom in an effort to get away from it all and have a moment to myself to feel my feelings. After smearing the wet tears from my face, a dragon-like sigh of relief exhaled from my chest. I was ready to go back home. My feelings of homesickness became sandwiched with gratitude for everything both sides of my family had done for me. The emotional journey this experience was taking me on had me feeling every peak and valley. I felt humbled. Pensive. Irritated. Complete. Vulnerable. Tired. Grateful. Hopeful. Invigorated. I needed to get home so I could wrap myself in familiarity and process this in its entirety. It just so happened that as I was finding myself, I was also losing a version of myself.

* * *

The next day, Antonio, his girlfriend, my parents and I spent the day downtown. First on the itinerary, my dad had scheduled a visit to the sister office of the company he works for in the United States. It was endearing to watch the excitement wash over his face as he compared the work his company does in Bogotá to his work back home. The office staff were great hosts. They served us coffee and smiles and insisted on taking pictures together. After our office visit, we hit the streets again to explore more of the downtown area. We then walked past The Halifax, the hotel where my parents stayed in 1990 when they adopted me. That hotel became a second home for them as they completed the tedious and emotional adoption process. We stood outside staring at a building that housed our new beginning as a family. My dad pointed at the window and said, "That room right there is where you spent the first part of your life with us." My emotionally drained heart skipped a few beats. Before I could sink into a tearful nostalgia, my mom urged us to find a spot for lunch. Ironically, the restaurant was called Crepes and Waffles. This Americanized restaurant felt apropos; our prelude to returning home to the United States. And like true *gringos*, we spent the rest of the afternoon shopping.

We returned to the house around sundown. When my birth mom saw me, she began to cry. Our time together during this visit was coming to an end and emotions were running high. I cozied up next to her on the couch and opened a translator app on my phone. I typed out how grateful I was that she put me up for adoption. I shared that this one defining act was the most loving gift anyone had ever given me. I told her that I had lived a very good life with an abundance of love, food, shelter, and opportunity. Her selfless decision was the real catalyst to every shining gem in my life. I hoped the translator was capturing the true essence of these words in a way that made sense. In that moment, I desperately needed her to understand the depths of my gratitude.

I also needed to break the news to Sara that I would be leaving the next day. Even though she seemed disappointed (and made some adorable sad faces), she understood. I felt a pang of regret that I hadn't spent more time with Santiago. We had a few genuine sibling experiences during this visit (like a good ol' fashioned Mortal Kombat video game battle) but he felt distant overall. As Vincente came to pick up Santiago, María, and Sara, I reached for Santiago and told him I loved him. He didn't say it back. Feelings of upset wrapped like a lasso around my chest. I hoped our goodbye at the airport tomorrow would resolve this hanging tension. I had started my tour of farewells when Antonio informed me that I would need to say goodbye to Santiago now, as he wouldn't be joining us at the airport in the morning. I turned to Santiago and pulled him into a hug, opening my heart once more to tell him how much I loved him. We held on for a long time as I cried. And to my surprise, so did he.

As we let go of our embrace, Santiago looked at me and said, " *Yo también* " ("I love you, too") We looked around at our family, who had been watching - and weeping - as we shared a final moment of vulnerability. With her childlike timing, Sara sprang into the room and shattered the tension. She put on a pouty show about me leaving that transformed our tears to laughter. She is magical in this way.

CHAPTER FOURTEEN
Departing

After putting in all the emotional labor it took to say goodbye, my parents' and my departing flight was canceled. I had been itching to go home, but I reveled in the idea of one more day with my complete family. I wanted the comforts of my American life but wasn't truly ready to leave. Not just yet.

The following day would be an easy-going one. We sprawled. We watched TV. We cuddled on the couch. And finally, we ate breakfast. I piddled around packing my suitcase to get it out of the way. Sara joined me as I put on my makeup. I caught glances of her pretending to do her own. I was so glad to have entered her life while she was so young. I could now be a part of her childhood memories. I hoped one day we would live under the same roof and reminisce about these special days we shared.

After finishing our sisterly makeup session, we went downstairs where my parents were meeting my Tío Jaime, the last of *Nonita*'s children they had yet to be introduced to. I watched as they received their proper Colombian greeting of kisses on the cheek. These kisses are no joke. Even if someone leaves the house for 15 minutes, when they come back inside, they are kissed all over again. And my parents would experience many more of them now that we had an extra day.

After meeting my Tío, my parents, Felipe, Antonio, Antonio's girlfriend and I went to two malls. And, finally, I discovered the secret to a Colombian woman's curves: *fajas* (shapewear). While I refused to admit this to any of my friends in Georgia, I purchased one at the mall so I could join Colombian women in their fantasy scenario of eating delicious food while looking like living hourglasses.

Once we got back to the house, I felt an urge to isolate myself and wrap up in the comfort of solitude, but I resisted. I stayed downstairs to spend my last few hours with my birth family. My birth mother informed me that she would be taking *Nonito* to the doctor tomorrow, and so we would not see her in the morning before we left. My mom and I exchanged knowing glances and gave her the last bit of Colombian pesos we had. It totaled around $120 U.S. dollars. We began our second round of goodbyes, this time skipping the tears. I showered Sara in a million kisses and then watched as she hugged my parents goodbye...four times each. My lack of emotional response caught me off guard.

I told my birth mother that I planned to return soon. Many of our conversations during my visit had been peppered with the question, "When are you coming back?" and every time I would tell her that I didn't know. Because I didn't. I knew I needed to do everything in my power to provide her with opportunities for comfort and happiness. If anyone deserved it, she did. And my return to Colombia could maybe provide that. But for now, her face sat heavy with sadness.

* * *

I was ready to go home. I needed a hot shower in my own room. I wanted to get wet gooey kisses from my dog Bella. I looked forward to sharing my collection of pictures and souvenirs with my brothers and friends. I knew I had a smorgasbord of feelings to unpack, but I was actually looking forward to doing so.

Our goodbyes during that final morning were even more anticlimactic. We had already cycled through so much emotion that I was left feeling only relief. I was glad that my parents had been able to connect with the people who share my blood. The full picture of my identity and our family's history had united. Our individual stories and quirks were woven together to create one big, beautiful family. As I prepared to go to the airport, I began recognizing just how much I had gained in the last two weeks.

Antonio and Tío Pepe brought my parents and me to the airport early in the morning and stayed with us until we got to security. I wondered when we would see them again. The idea of not knowing was unsettling but I chose to stay present and enjoy our last moments together. When it was time to say goodbye, we hugged once more and thanked them for their hospitality. My parents and I turned around several times to wave goodbye as we made our way through security to the plane's gate. As we settled into our seats on the plane, I looked out of the window and watched as the Colombian men used their signal wands to direct the plane toward the runway. I was *actually* leaving. The reality sunk in as we took off. I reflected back to the first time I landed in Colombia and how much fear, excitement and nervousness I had experienced. The memory brought a smile to my face. I turned away from the window to watch as my parents grabbed each other's hands. Their unconditional love and unending support was so great that it pulled me in through osmosis. *I'm a lucky girl.*

As we ascended into the clouds, I peeked out of my window and took in the majesty of a bird's eye view of Colombia. I could see the collage of multicolored roofs and car-filled streets as we climbed into the sky. Green and brown pastures dissolved into one another until the view was engulfed by a bright whiteness. *I love so many people below these clouds.* I reflected on the relationships I had formed and wondered if they were simultaneously imagining me in the sky above them. Perhaps my birth family felt a crumb of the pain my birth mother felt when she watched as I was taken away from her as a newborn baby.

As the flight wore on, a one-year-old boy began making a racket across the aisle. I did my best to politely ignore him. As we landed in Atlanta, my mom struck up a conversation with the boy's mother. The woman had just adopted the boy from Colombia. The moment he stepped off the plane, he would be well on his way to becoming an American citizen. The hairs on my arms shot upward. What were the chances? I saw him through new eyes. This was just the beginning for him.

That wasn't the only exciting part of my journey home. Sitting directly beside the little boy was the famous Colombian actor, Andrés Parra. Andrés, too, seemed irritated by the restless child. Once he overheard our conversation about adoption, he perked up and smiled at the boy. We were all feeling the love.

The cultural shift I felt when I touched down in America was palpable. People were less welcoming. I tried not to make sweeping conclusions about Americans, but the people in Atlanta's airport that day were not helping. Overtly privileged children were glued to their smartphones, people shuffled angrily to and fro, and giant distances separated every human body from one other. *Heaven forbid anyone accidentally bump elbows with a stranger in line.*

Friendly exchanges seemed few and far between. Was the society that raised me one of ingratitude? I hoped not. If these lines would have been full of Colombian people, there would be smiling, talking, story swapping, and no complaints. Frustration seemed to ping pong from one traveler to another. I kept contrasting the U.S. and Colombia. And then it hit me.

My country of birth had won my heart. I already missed the ever-present sense of humility that lingers over dinner tables and busy shopping malls. I missed the zest for life, no matter the setting. Nothing goes to waste in Colombia, least of all an opportunity to celebrate the present moment.

My Colombian friend Juan planned to give us a ride home from the airport. It just so happened that his car died in the parking lot and his friend, a Mexican taxi driver, was available to drive us home instead. Although we were back in Atlanta, we were once again crammed into the backseat of a taxi doing our best to decipher the language of our driver. We all shook our heads and laughed. *Still going with the flow*, I thought. It was the perfect homecoming.

CHAPTER FIFTEEN
Readjusting

That wet, sloppy kiss I wanted from my dog Bella? I got plastered with it the second I walked in the front door of my house. After my canine love fest, I made a beeline for our kitchen sink. I grabbed a glass from the cabinet, filled it to the brim with water, and chugged. Clean, free-flowing drinking water saturated my tired body. And not a plastic bottle in sight. After quenching what felt like a three-week thirst, I went upstairs to take a hot shower. I gleefully watched steam pour over the shower curtain and crawl across the bathroom floor. I indulged in every warm drip that touched my skin. I basked in the gratitude of having the luxury of choosing my shower's temperature. Before turning the shower off, I changed the water temperature to cold. I closed my eyes and imagined I was showering at Tío Fidel's house in Guadalupe after a day spent at the pool under the hot sun. I could almost hear Sara's faint giggles coming from down the hall. The water's icy sting brought me back home for just a moment.

As I stepped out of the shower, my feet settled on carpet. I realized I had never seen carpet during my time in Colombia. My feet enjoyed the springy plush path to the closet, where I was reminded of my excessive American lifestyle. I felt guilty for having so much when the people I love have so little. It didn't seem fair.

The more I reflected on the differences between life in the U.S. and life in Colombia, the more I began to contemplate what it means to have true freedom. When we visited the Bogotá office of my dad's company, we met a man who offered us his unique perspective. He had once lived in the States, where he purchased a home near a soccer field so his son could play whenever he wanted. After they settled into their new home, his family was informed that the soccer field was private and thus his son was not allowed to use it. A liability issue, they were told. He explained, through obvious resentment, that life in the United States - "the land of the free" - is riddled with strict rules and regulations. It was enough to send that man and his family back to Bogotá.

This made me think. If my birth family ever moved to the U.S., I would need to watch their every move as they acclimated to daily life. Perhaps one day I would be able to afford a house in the city where they could stay and get around via public transportation or on foot. That would feel like home for them. Maybe I could help my birth mom open a Colombian restaurant in Atlanta. My daydreaming continued until reality hit: I needed to get to work. While waiting tables part-time at a Cuban restaurant might not seem glamorous, I was excited to save every penny I could. I had dreams for my future and for my family. Every dollar earned brought me closer to those dreams.

* * *

Being back home took more adjusting than I expected. While I anticipated waves of intense emotion, it felt instead like I was running through the motions. I journaled constantly to see if I could sort through these mixed-up feelings. My first bits of introspection brought forth waves of indebtedness. How could my life be any more blessed? I was living with my parents in an affluent city. Everything felt easy and simple. Meanwhile in those same moments, my birth family was hundreds of miles away working tirelessly to make ends meet. The world was at my feet and I still couldn't seem to find my footing.

This uneasiness brought me a new perspective on all the strangers I interact with each day. I don't know anything about their personal journeys or what experiences they are processing. Sheltered and naive, a younger Mariela didn't give other people's perspectives this much thought. Evolved and learning, the new Mariela would extend grace and compassion to everyone she met. I felt invigorated. I wanted to make a greater positive impact. I wanted to be influential. I wanted to celebrate my story and everything the future held.

With this future vision in tow, I set out to face the one thing I had been putting off since I returned home. As we were preparing to leave Colombia, each of my parents wrote my birth mom a letter. I took a picture of them on my phone so I could have a copy before they gave them to María. I hadn't yet read them. It was time. I felt them calling to me from my phone's photo album. I wanted to read my mom's first. I was ready to see the words written by the mother of my heart to the mother of my blood.

Dear María,

I am so happy that I was able to meet you. I have always had all my children's birth mothers close to my heart and in my prayers. However, when I have thought of you, I have felt a special connection that I could never explain. Now I know I was meant to meet you. I have always had you in my thoughts especially on holidays and Mariela's birthdays. I always wished I could contact you and let you know Mariela was safe and loved. Also, when I thought of you, I felt your pain. I know I can't take away your pain from the past but hope I can make the present happier for you.

I can see Mariela's happiness and that she now feels complete to have found you. Thank you for being so strong to bring her into your life and that of your family. Thank you for bringing us into your family, as well. We are so happy to have met Santiago, Sara, and Vincente. We feel we have another family who we love and who we feel loved by. I can see what a wonderful mother you are! Sara and Santiago are wonderful people! Our story (yours, Mari's, Pete's and mine) is very special and will bond us forever. I want you to know we love you and your whole family. You are always welcome in our home as you are a part of our family. We will visit as much as we can. God bless you.

Love,

Lisa

Next, I read the letter from my dad.

Dear María,

I am happy that we could meet you and your wonderful family in Colombia! Santiago is a good young man who has a heart of gold. Sara is so cute and intelligent. And, from the story Mari told us about how you met Vincente, he is an angel here on Earth.

Mari has always been interested in finding you. When she started searching a year or two ago, I was afraid she would be disappointed -- either by not finding her birth mother or perhaps by rejection. However, I am very happy that things worked out as they did. I see many of your features and personality in Mariela. I am so glad we could meet you. I hope that you feel the same. I cannot imagine the uncertainty you must have felt for over 20 years. I wish you could have known that she was safe and growing up with a lot of love. I hope you now have peace and you are comforted to see what a beautiful and intelligent young woman she has grown to be. I hope you will not feel guilt, but rather that Mari has had many opportunities in life and that she has made us very happy and fulfilled to have her in our lives. We hope that we can continue to meet and visit with you and your family in the future.

Best wishes and much love,

Pete

My heart pounded a drum solo in my chest. The words my mother chose, and their rhythm and sequence reminded me of how the universe orchestrates everything far beyond our immediate knowledge. I always thought of my birth mother on my birthday and I had always felt a tethered connection to her without explanation. From a young age, I desired to give her peace but when I imagined her thinking of me, I sensed pain. It was fascinating to know that my mom felt the same way. A part of me believed that this shared love and empathy created a force strong enough to bring us together in person.

When I read about the connection my mom felt to my birth mother, my heart swelled. What a loving woman mom is. She had enough compassion to express her love and gratitude for the woman who gave me life. We both wanted to offer María peace. We both wanted her to be happy. I always assumed my passion was a Colombian characteristic. After reading my mom's letter, I realized that I inherited *mi corazon grande* (my big heart) from *two* women whose big hearts are filled with unconditional love.

Every letter and word of my dad's note wrapped me in his unique brand of love. It takes a strong man to embark on a journey to Colombia to meet his daughter's biological family. And it takes a great man to express himself to them in the way that he did in his letter. The stark contrast between the mysteries of my birth father and the known attributes of my dad became vividly clear. Tangled up in sentiment, I closed my eyes and prayed that I would one day find a man as equally loving and kind as my father.

CHAPTER SIXTEEN
Connecting

The culmination of my adventures could be summarized in one word: home. Growing up in Georgia, home was a Norman Rockwell painting: a suburban life filled with material comfort and routine convenience. My Colombian adventures taught me that home is as immaterial as love. Despite language barriers, cultural divides, and heightened levels of discomfort, I felt more at home in Colombia than I could have imagined. I learned how intention, flow, vulnerability and love can make the world your home. By using these inherent tools, we are all capable of connecting to the universal heart. My birth family and I were complete strangers when we met, yet we threw ourselves off a precipice of emotional uncertainty hoping, praying, wishing it would result in lifelong connection. And because we did, we found family in each other. We found in one another a source of unyielding love.

While I was able to put the most essential pieces of my family puzzle together, there were still missing pieces I was yearning to pursue. I needed to continue my quest, no evidence left undiscovered. For every missing piece I filled in with family, I filled a missing piece within myself.

Being adopted, and the process of finding my biological family, has been complex and layered. In order to partake in this journey, I had to succumb to piercing vulnerability. I was asked to relinquish control. I was forced to dissolve preconceived notions and unrealistic expectations. The process of letting go connected me more deeply to my spiritual beliefs. Without a road map in hand, I relied on a faith-powered navigation system to light my way. Connecting to the hearts of my family members led me to connect to the universal heart that's accessible to all of us. I now see that divine timing placed me exactly where I needed to be when I needed to be there. I discovered that humankind's true beauty surfaces when we disregard geographical and cultural differences and recognize our innate similarities. We were not born to look at other human beings as separate from us, but rather as equal and necessary components to the greatness we become when we unite. I've learned that the phrase "Home is where the heart is" is actually quite true, but it's not about a location at all. It's a feeling, a sense of belonging. When people open their hearts to one another, a sense of home can be found. My heart and my identity could no longer belong to a dot on a map.

I am more than American.

I am more than Colombian.

I am human.

And I am proud.

Mariela's Colombian family at the airport
waiting to meet her for the first time.

Mariela and her biological mother
María

Mariela and her sister Sara

Mariela's brother Santiago and
her

Pete, Lisa, Mariela, María and Sara at the airport after introducing Mariela's parents to María for the first time.

Mariela Andersen was adopted from Bogotá Colombia as an infant and grew up in Alpharetta GA with her parents and two brothers. In 2012 she traveled to Colombia to meet her biological family and has traveled to Colombia seven times since then. She graduated from Valdosta State University in 2014 with her bachelor's degree in American Sign Language Interpretation. Mariela has been working in public education interpreting for Deaf and Hard of Hearing students for five and a half years. Mariela is a certified Yoga instructor for children. She enjoys practicing yoga, going to the beach, spending time with family, working with kids and making art. She lives in Marietta Georgia with her Brazilian husband Philippe and Cairn Terrier named Ella. You can follow more of her journey on her Instagram page @marielaandersenn

Made in the USA
Columbia, SC
20 September 2021